What people are saying about …

GOD KNOWS MY NAME

"Reading *God Knows My Name* has been an absolute joy! It's amazing how freedom, healing, and relief come over our hearts as we hear again how much God loves us and embraces us in spite of our choices or past. His plan of hope for us is sure. We can praise Him in the midst of all of life's craziness knowing our dependence and hope in Him will never be disappointed."

Shelley Giglio, chief strategist for Passion
Conferences and director of Label Operations
and Artist Management for sixstepsrecords

"In *God Knows My Name*, Beth Redman writes candidly and hopefully about her journey from the shadows into God's healing light. Beth writes like she lives, with conviction, passion, clarity, and a desire to see others face their past and present struggles as loved children of a perfect heavenly Father. *God Knows My Name* is filled with truth that transforms and the power that makes all things new. I can't wait for you to dive into its pages and allow God to totally revolutionize your life."

Louie Giglio, pastor of Passion City Church
and founder of the Passion Movement

"Our beautiful friend Beth has always had a stunning gift for communicating the heart of God toward humanity, and in *God Knows My Name*, she has done it again. To hear such an honest account of a journey to wholeness is completely inspiring, as how and where we gain our sense of personal value is one of life's great definers. So thank you, Beth, for allowing us all a glimpse into your heart, and we thank God for the solution that will be the ultimate result of this wonderful book."

Darlene Zschech, lead worshipper,
songwriter, and author

"This book beautifully depicts the redemptive heart of our God. In her very own down-to-earth and fun writing style, Beth Redman shares how she discovered the Father's heart in the midst of overcoming trials and difficult circumstances. Using biblical and real-life examples, she will guide you into a journey of restoration where wholeness and freedom become yours."

Lisa Bevere, best-selling author and
speaker, Messenger International

GOD KNOWS
MY NAME

GOD KNOWS MY NAME

NEVER FORGOTTEN, FOREVER LOVED

BETH REDMAN

transforming lives together

GOD KNOWS MY NAME
Published by David C. Cook
4050 Lee Vance View
Colorado Springs, CO 80918 U.S.A.

David C. Cook Distribution Canada
55 Woodslee Avenue, Paris, Ontario, Canada N3L 3E5

David C. Cook U.K., Kingsway Communications
Eastbourne, East Sussex BN23 6NT, England

Survivor is an imprint of David C. Cook
Kingsway Communications Ltd
info@survivor.co.uk

David C. Cook and the graphic circle C logo
are registered trademarks of Cook Communications Ministries.

All rights reserved. Except for brief excerpts for review purposes,
no part of this book may be reproduced or used in any form
without written permission from the publisher.

All Scripture quotations, unless otherwise noted, are taken from the *Holy Bible,
New International Version*®. *NIV*®. Copyright © 1973, 1978, 1984 by International
Bible Society. Used by permission of Zondervan. All rights reserved. Scripture
quotations marked MSG are taken from *THE MESSAGE*. Copyright © by Eugene
Peterson 1993, 1994, 1995, 1996, 2000, 2001, 2002. Used by permission of
NavPress Publishing Group. Scripture quotations marked AB are taken from
The Amplified Bible. Copyright © 1954, 1958, 1962, 1964, 1965, 1987 by The
Lockman Foundation. Used by permission. All rights reserved. Scripture quotations
marked NLT are taken from the New Living Translation of the Holy Bible. New
Living Translation copyright © 1996, 2004 by Tyndale Charitable Trust. Used by
permission of Tyndale House Publishers. Scripture quotations marked ESV are taken
from the *Holy Bible, English Standard Version*. Copyright © 2000; 2001 by Crossway
Bibles, a division of Good News Publishers. Used by permission. All rights reserved.
Scripture quotations marked NKJV are taken from the New King James Version.
Copyright © 1982 by Thomas Nelson, Inc. Used by permission. All rights reserved.
Scripture quotations marked KJV are from the King James Version of the Bible.
Public Domain. The author has added italics to Scripture quotations for emphasis.

LCCN 2010926417
ISBN 978-0-7814-0365-8
eISBN 978-0-7814-0489-1

© 2010 Beth Redman

The Team: Don Pape, Alex Field, Amy Kiechlin, Caitlyn York, Karen Athen
Cover design: Sarah Schultz
Cover image: iStockphoto, royalty free

Printed in the United States of America
First Edition 2010

1 2 3 4 5 6 7 8 9 10

042910

To Grace Shaw, Beth Hawthorne, and Georgia Pennells:
You three beautiful girls were my teeny-tiny bridesmaids
all those years ago! Now you have blossomed into three
stunning girls of God. I pray you will use your gifts
and shine your light—you have an amazing future
ahead of you, and I cannot wait to see how God uses
you in the days and years to come! Keep seeking, keep
shining, but most of all keep loving Him, always!

Much love,

Beth

CONTENTS

ACKNOWLEDGMENTS

Julie Wanstall—Thank you for carrying this project with me and for your invaluable input. You have been honest, encouraging, sharpening, and inspiring throughout. We all know I could not have started or finished this book without your incredible hard work, support, and brilliant editing! Thank you does not seem enough, Julie. I love you dearly and cannot wait for all that lies ahead!

Matt Redman—for who you are when no one's looking and for your incredible love for me, our children, and, most importantly, for our God. Redders, I simply adore you.

Maisey-Ella, Noah, Rocco, Jackson, and Levi—how blessed can one woman be?! You are absolutely amazing and the joy of my life. Run with all you've got; God has amazing plans for your life!

Louie and Shelley Giglio and Passion City Church—we love you, and we are humbled to know you as friends and to have been on this amazing journey in Atlanta with you.

Robin and Denise—my precious Atlanta soul sisters! Thank you for your love, prayers, and incredible covering. I love you so much!

And to dear and faithful friends—Martin and Anna Smith—friends like no other.

David and Carrie Grant; Mike Pilavachi; Gary Richardson; Anna De Filippo; Matt and Natasha Robinson; Jonas Myrin; Christa Black; Lisa Bevere (Mama Lioness!); Mike and Tasha Shaw; Frog and Amy Orr-Ewing; my dear mum and mum-in-law, Lesley Vickers and Barbara Redman; and the entire Redman family—I am so grateful for you all!

Also, thanks to Kelly Moreton, Lindsay Jernigan, and Julianna Lopes, who support us in the most practical and life-changing ways.

And I send my heartfelt appreciation to David C. Cook—thank you to Don Pape; my incredible editor, Alex Field; and the whole team for believing in this book and supporting me throughout the process. I am so blessed and privileged to be on this journey with you all. Thank you so very much.

And finally to God the Father—I am Yours forevermore.

—Beth Redman

FOREWORD

I have known Beth and Matt Redman for many years as valued friends, and I am delighted to write the foreword to this book.

As you read this book, you will hear a woman talking bravely and honestly about some of the most difficult times in her life. Yet this is not one of those books that we can fit onto the bookshop shelves so depressingly headed "Tragic Life Stories." It is not such a book for three reasons.

First of all, Beth has resisted the temptation to wallow in the misery and pain she has known. Well done, Beth, for letting the past be the past and not sawing sawdust!

Second, this is not a tragic book, but a triumphant one; Beth points beyond personal suffering to the healing of God's grace in Christ. In this book is a contagious, bubbling amazement at the awesome power, presence, peace, and grace of a God who not only knows our individual names, but also loves us more than we can ever understand. To know the truth of that is truly liberating and healing.

And third, this is a profoundly practical teaching book. Beth writes not to settle scores or to engage in emotional self-therapy, but to share lessons learned along the journey in the school of hard knocks to help others. There is page after page of helpful reflections, insights, and wise guidance as Beth lays out the reasons why it's possible to be encouraged and uplifted as we trust in God.

I know many people will be enriched, inspired, and helped by this dynamic book. I am one of them, and you surely will be too.

—J.John

www.philotrust.com

Chapter One

God Knows My Name

Our parents are often broken people wearing big learner's plates, like drivers in training, when we arrive in their world. We shouldn't judge them harshly, but sometimes the parents we need to love us the most can hurt us and let us down.

As a mum, I take it very personally and get a little feisty when my daughter, Maisey-Ella, is bullied or mistreated. I consider it outrageous when I know someone has hurt her, and I find it hard not to intervene. My husband has told me on many occasions, "You can't give little girls evil looks, Beth!" My daughter is, quite simply, utterly gorgeous inside and out. Of course she is not perfect, but the problem all of us face is that the world is not going to like us, love us, or be on our side all of the time. Some days we will be misunderstood, blamed, and rejected. But in our home, when Maisey-Ella returns from a miserable day at school, two pairs of loving arms wait for her. Arms that without question are available to wipe away any tear, and hearts of love that speak gentle words of acceptance, reassurance, and a promise that no matter what … we love you, beautiful girl, and *we are for you*.

Every single human being needs the comfort and reassurance that on the days the tears fall—even if the "world" rejects us—the people who really know us (warts and all) will be there for us. Those people are our parents, our family. Sometimes, though, our family isn't there.

However, God is an ever-present, all-loving, all-forgiving, amazing Father in heaven. He can override imperfect parenting, soothe any broken spirit, and free any bound-up heart.

I want to tell you my story.

I want to share an amazing story of restoration, a story of the hope that we all have and the truth that I pray will fill you with joy, freedom, and power! I'm not pointing the finger at anyone or trying to make anyone look bad. I simply want to shout out that God heals, restores, has plans for you, and *utterly adores you!* If we can truly breathe in that truth, we become free to live, free to give, and free to love and accept both others and ourselves. Then, as you breathe that truth out into a hurting and broken world that desperately needs this message of God the Father's heart for us, God is glorified, and lives are changed and transformed by Him.

My mum was a true saint when I was growing up, and my closest friend. She brought me to church and taught me about God. In public my dad seemed the perfect father, but in private he struggled with anger … and we suffered terrible violence. In my very late teens my parents separated. I don't think we should place our parents' mistakes or faults under the microscope and blame them for all our problems and baggage. God teaches us to forgive, and He gives us the grace to do so. He enables us to rise above the harshest of circumstances and to begin again. He rewrites generations of brokenness to give us an incredible hope and future with Jesus.

But I want to tell this story because I believe in a God who restores, and through His power I have seen reconciliation and healing occur in the most broken of families. I know it is possible, and I have always prayed for that with my own father. However, it takes more than just a miracle for that to happen—it also requires the openness and humility of all involved. Since my parents divorced, my dad and I have had sporadic contact. Throughout that time I found it impossible and even destructive to have a normal father-daughter relationship, so I have walked carefully and lived my adult life without him.

During my pregnancy with our third child, I began to have some worrying symptoms, and after the baby's birth, doctors began to test me for suspected liver disease. The specialist I was seeing told me that, before my liver biopsy, he needed to know as much about my medical background as possible. He asked me to contact all my living relatives and find out if anyone in the family had ever had liver problems. I contacted each family member and very nervously sent an email to my dad. He wrote back immediately, and still to this day I cannot believe his parting words.

He wrote that, yes, there was liver disease in the family, and also cancer, and he hoped I had both.

"Beth," he wrote, "you deserve to suffer, because suffering would make someone as egotistical and vile as you a better person."

Wow.

He also threw in some awful comments about Matt and our children that need not be repeated. The email ended with him telling me I was cut out of his will and he had instructed his solicitor never to disclose his death or where he would be buried. While I was waiting for news of my liver condition, my earthly father had just cursed me and condemned my life.

God made us to love and to be loved. My earthly dad knew me, rejected me, and also detested me. Could anything be more painful?

I could hardly breathe. I phoned Matt and read him the email. I called my mum and my best friend, Anna. Inside I was crying out, *Someone tell me I am loved! Please take away the pain of this horrific rejection*—the words had gone so deep it felt as though my inmost parts were bleeding. I was desperate for a deeper love, validation, and acceptance. No human words could soothe me.

I put down the phone and gasped for air.

I cried out to my God … my *true,* amazing Father, my *heavenly,* forever Father, the One who knows all my failures and shortcomings and yet has *never ever* rejected me. He wrote my name on the palms of His hands and He stretched out His arms, and as He was viciously nailed to a cross, He separated me from my sin forever and loved me enough to die unjustly. He walked a journey of horrific agony—pleading, being taunted—and He carried my cross, my death, my past, and my sin. His love was enough as He cried out, "It is finished!" So now death and pain, brokenness and rejection, where are your sting? Everything I ever need in life is now accessible and available to me through His death.

Our God is a God who saves and who accepts and who can heal us completely. His love outweighed the words of a wounded man whose own life was so broken that he knew only how to crush others. I faced up to the pain of the situation, but at the same time knew a beautiful and powerful revelation that spoke louder than all of those other words: Though my father may forsake me, my God will never reject me. Though my earthly dad may try to erase me from his life, I shall never be forgotten. In that moment I knew a deep and permanent truth covering over the whole of my life: that God *knows my name.*

My Father in heaven adores me, has plans to prosper me and supernatural arms to hold me. He is with me by His Spirit every time a situation threatens to overwhelm and whenever I want to hide away and give in to the insecure, evil thoughts that come knocking. My God would never reject or forget me. He did not forget me in my time of need. From heaven He called out to me reminding me that I am His! Because He made me, He *knows* me, and He loves me! I am His forever. God spoke to me powerfully from His Word:

> *Can a mother forget the baby at her breast and*
> *have no compassion on the child she has borne?*
> *Though she may forget, I will not forget you! See,*
> *I have engraved you on the palms of my hands.*
> *(Isa. 49:15–16)*

You are known by name by the Living God, the loving heavenly Father. He made you, He redeemed you, He hears you, and never ever will He forget you. Hallelujah!

In this book I want to share with you some of the powerful ways that God helped me overrule such a massive rejection with His glorious eternal truth. I hope this can help you in your own life and enable you to help others.

Isaiah 43:1–4 says this:

> *But now, this is what the LORD says—*
> *he who created you, O Jacob,*

he who formed you, O Israel:
"Fear not, for I have redeemed you;
I have summoned you by name; you are mine.

When you pass through the waters,
I will be with you;
and when you pass through the rivers,
they will not sweep over you.
When you walk through the fire,
you will not be burned;
the flames will not set you ablaze.

For I am the LORD, your God,
the Holy One of Israel, your Savior....

Since you are precious and honored in my sight,
and because I love you."

In this passage, there are several truths for us to grasp, which I want to break down and look at one by one in this chapter.

God Knows Your Name

"I have summoned you by name; you are mine." (Isa. 43:1)

A name is given and considered. A name imparts meaning, value, identity, and significance. Your name was chosen specifically, and especially, for you. A name gives both humanity and dignity to a person. The Enemy would have you live a *nameless* existence— feeling anonymous, illegitimate, unknown, unimportant, inglorious, and unfit to be named. Nineteenth-century London was a time of such material, emotional, and spiritual poverty that "children were so utterly uncared for that some were even without names, and were known to each other by nicknames."[1]

In direct contrast, God says that He has a name for us. Where we feel worthless and insignificant He bestows worth and significance upon us when He calls us by name and chooses us for His glory.

Anyone expecting a child has flipped through baby-name books, looking at the meanings and origins of names and thinking about how they sound. I've found names I loved and then been dismayed to find out they meant something like *harlot, wench,* or *crooked nose!*

Someone recently told me of a child who had been named Jezebel Harlot! That's a pretty negative connotation to speak over a child every time she is called. Ideally, a name needs to suit the person carrying it. When my husband suggested that we name our third child "Rocco Redman," I thought he had gone a bit mad! Normally my husband's track record in making decisions is spot on. There really is no point arguing with Mr. Matthew Redman because over the years I have found he is nearly always right. However, on this occasion, I wasn't so sure.

I wanted our third child to be called Benjamin, but Matt got the older children on board—and in the end I came to peace with the fact that if he was anything like his dad and his brother and sister, he would easily live up to something as strong and bold as Rocco! The name means "rest," and so far he has turned out to be the most relaxed, peaceful, deep-sleeping, and gentle-spirited boy … and he has the confidence and joy required to be *Rocco Redman*. In new environments, his name still causes a little reaction, but it is so perfect for him, and I love that every time I write or call him by his full name, Rocco Benjamin Courage, I am affirming and speaking *rest, sonship, bravery,* and *boldness* over him.

In the same way, your Father God named you as precious, chosen, and beloved. You may not be named Rocco, but when God calls you, He speaks over you His truth, freedom, and life. Your part is to make a good choice—to continually believe and live under those things He named you and never to seek to hide behind another name. Many of us each day live under other labels that the Enemy has given us from past or present experiences—unwanted, failure, doubter, ugly, unlovely, needy, drama queen, mistake, disgrace, shamed, forgotten, and many more lies.

Those thoughts and feelings cannot possibly originate from God—for He is the giver of good and perfect gifts, and the God of all comfort. Those negative impressions of yourself and the words my own dad wrote in his email to me originate from the Enemy—who we know to be a dirty liar.

Perhaps you think your problems and insecurities are too great to overcome. By the kindness and mercy of God in my own life, I can assure you that this is not the case. I was abused physically, put down verbally, and rejected. I suffered humiliation many times and sadly began to act out how I felt about myself. In public I felt wretchedly insecure. I couldn't go out with friends without feeling self-conscious and unimportant. I hated myself inside and out.

Then Jesus called my name. And everything changed. I hardly recognize the person I was back then. Our names may conjure up memories, but not always truth. I know that ultimately I am defined not by what others think of me when they hear my name, or what my earthly father says about me. Instead, the authority and compassion of the God who called my name define me. He loves, He shapes, He convicts, and He lavishes us with affirmation.

It's time we heard His voice the loudest.

God Made Me

This is what the LORD *says—*
He who created you, O Jacob,
He who formed you, O Israel. (Isa. 43:1)

Part of understanding the depths of God's knowledge of us lies in grasping the importance of the fact that He made us.

Psalm 139:13–14 puts it beautifully:

> *For you created my inmost being;*
> > *you knit me together in my mother's womb.*

> *I praise you because I am fearfully and*
> > *wonderfully made;*
> > *your works are wonderful,*
> > *I know that full well.*

The phrase *inmost being* is literally translated "kidneys." In Hebrew idiom this meant the innermost center of the emotions and the moral sensitivity of a person's heart.[2] Here we see that God does not just know us as a casual acquaintance or simply acknowledge our existence, marvelous though that would be for the God of heaven to do such a thing. Rather, He knows who we are right down to the final detail. God knows how you work, how you think, what makes you happy, what makes you sad. He knows the last time you cried, and what you cried about. He knows what you would like for your birthday, and He actually cares about it too. The amazing thing is you don't actually have to tell Him all of this. He just knows, because He made you, He sees you, He hears you, and He loves you. He knows you better than you know yourself.

He knows what you need before a word is even spoken from your mouth or articulated in your heart.

God Speaks Worth Over Me

*"Since you are precious and honored in my sight,
and because I love you." (Isa. 43:4)*

The first thing God said when He looked at His creation was, "It is good." The very fact that God made you means you are wonderful!

The psalmist declares: "Your works are wonderful, I know that full well" (Ps. 139:14). Yet God didn't just make you, then say, "What a great job," and leave you on a shelf. No, He pursues a relationship with you, He gives His life for you, that He may know you daily, deeply, and eternally.

Just before we were married, Matt received an invitation from Buckingham Palace. When Matt read the guest list he was a little intimidated. Top sports personalities, journalists, and film stars— *and my fiancé!* When he eventually met the Queen, along with Prince Charles, Matt performed a fumbled bow and stood back in shock. That was the *Queen!*

He couldn't believe he had been chosen to hold out his hand and meet her majesty face-to-face. Somehow Matt had been deemed worthy of a moment with the Queen and her son, and he felt truly humbled. What a privilege!

Yet the truth is that there is a higher honor—a more amazing invitation that lies open for all of us. God in heaven; the Lord of all creation; the God of Abraham, Isaac, and Jacob; the God of your pastor and your friends who are missionaries abroad; the God of Corrie ten Boom and Martin Luther; the Author of life; the Beginning and the End—He extends the hand of friendship to you! Just as Matt was invited to stand alongside celebrities and dignitaries before the Queen at Buckingham Palace, so too are we invited to stand before the God of heaven and earth as an equal alongside great heroes of the faith … and not just to meet Him but to *know* Him! He speaks His love and your worth loudly over you today.

Listen closely: Isaiah 61:3 says that He bestows on us "a *crown* of beauty instead of ashes," and Psalm 103:4 says that God "redeems your life from the pit and *crowns* you with love and compassion."

Anyone wearing a crown holds her head up high. She does not have an identity problem. She has been given honor and dignity.

God speaks worth over you. He declares His love for you. You are precious in His sight. Just like when I speak *rest, sonship,* and *courage*

over my child, every time God calls your name He speaks worth and
value over you. He knows you intimately because He made you, and
He loves you completely.

God Hears Me

"I am the LORD, *your God,*
the Holy One of Israel, your Savior." (Isa. 43:3)

It is a fundamental human need to be heard and understood. In
fact, if we feel that we are not heard, we feel a vast sense of loneliness
and emptiness. If we are not heard, we do not feel understood, and if
we do not feel understood, we will not feel known. The whole point
about God knowing our names, and about Him making us, is that
He knows us. When we discover that we are known and understood
by a friend, it can be profoundly moving. Sometimes a really good
friend may understand us better than we understand ourselves.

Tom Marshall, in his book *Right Relationships*, says that no one
can survive for long unless "we feel that somebody understands us,
somebody knows what we are feeling and somebody appreciates
our real desires and intentions."[3] And yet, however powerful being
known and understood by a friend or your partner can be, no one
can know you better or understand you more than God Himself.

Psalm 139:1–4 puts it magnificently:

O LORD, *you have searched me*
and you know me.

You know when I sit and when I rise;
you perceive my thoughts from afar.

You discern my going out and my lying down;
you are familiar with all my ways.

Before a word is on my tongue
you know it completely, O LORD.

Some people might find this depth of understanding quite frightening—and indeed there is always a risk attached to loving and being loved, knowing and being known. God knows us completely and utterly. Our thoughts, feelings, and emotions are an open book to God. He sees what we do, and He hears what we say even before we say it, or even when we're not talking to Him! He knows what you are doing and why you are doing it. More importantly, He knows your dreams, your ambitions, and your longings. But how can we know for ourselves that God really knows us in our inmost being, completely and utterly?

We know that we are known because *He hears us.*

When we know that God hears us, it transforms us from being fearful, doubting God's love, mercy, and goodness, into people who can be certain of His love for us. When God spoke to me through that song on my iPod, through the beautiful words of Isaiah 49, I knew that He had heard my cry—and He stepped in very powerfully at that moment, speaking His Word of life over me.

God was faithful to me through His real, tangible words of truth. I had a choice. I knew I did not have to believe my earthly father's words. My heavenly Father had seen my pain and had answered me in a deeply personal way from His Word.

God Has Not Forgotten Me

"When you pass through the waters,
I will be with you." (Isa. 43:2)

Sometimes we can know the truth of God in our minds, but not let it sink into our hearts. Or perhaps we have experienced a time of spiritual dryness, a time of suffering, or a time of God's silence. During these times, it can feel like God has forgotten us. This can be frightening and even cause us to question the truth and reality of God.

A friend recently told me that her current situation makes her feel as though she was five years old again and her father has forgotten to pick her up from school. That is a very real and deeply unsettling feeling, and it can shake our faith and our trust in God to the core. *My situation is telling me You are not here and You are not coming. Where are You, God?* Yet the true extent of God's care and concern for us is breathtaking:

> *"Are not five sparrows sold for two pennies? Yet*
> *not one of them is forgotten by God. Indeed,*
> *the very hairs of your head are all numbered.*
> *Don't be afraid; you are worth more than many*
> *sparrows." (Luke 12:6–7)*

God is not like your earthly father. Difficult circumstances do not mean He has failed or abandoned you. He has not left you at the school gate. God does not forget the child He made. He has not put you to one side while He is busy with other people. He is not bored with you, and He did not leave you midproject. He adores you. In fact, He promises (and God is incapable of breaking a promise) in Joshua 1:5, "I will never leave you nor forsake you." He continually watches over you. "He [takes] great delight in you, he will quiet you with his love, he will rejoice over you with singing" (Zeph. 3:17).

God is continually at pains to remind us not to be afraid, because He is with us. If He is with us, how can He forget us?

If you feel forgotten, I want to encourage you to believe the Word of God when He says, "I am with you always, to the very end of the age" (Matt. 28:20).

Call out to the Lord, and He will answer you. Wait patiently for the Lord, for He *will* turn to you and hear your cry. God loves you, He hears you, He speaks to you, and He *will* rescue you. Amen!

Chapter Two

GOD KNOWS MY PAST

I am so grateful to God that I grew up going to church. From a very early age I went to my local nondenominational church. I loved learning about God and couldn't wait for Sundays or the midweek youth club. When I look back I can see that was the awesome hand of God on my life, providing me with a chance to know Him and be a part of a beautiful community.

In the midst of a desert He put an amazing river beside me.

Brought up on a council estate, an area of government-funded housing, from an early age I saw things ranging from drugs and violence to prostitution. Yet by God's amazing grace, every Sunday I strolled down the hill and entered a place where love and freedom triumphed over poverty and oppression. For a few years we stopped going to church until, when I was eleven, my parents found a new church with a huge, vibrant youth group. Crawley Community Church had incredible leaders and teachers and a vibrant worship team. I experienced God in a powerful way, and I was reminded that because God sent His Son, Jesus, we are given the chance of a whole new life and a beautiful future.

But with a difficult home life and terrible self-esteem, which way would I go?

Even though I grew up in church and fully believed and trusted in Jesus, I would say that my teen years were a dark struggle between desperately wanting to follow God and dealing with the secret violence and abuse we lived with at home. I couldn't say anything, and this caused a huge conflict within me. My teenage heart was torn, battling between two causes. I loved Jesus, but I longed for the acceptance of others. I exhausted myself by singing one thing and going away and immediately pursuing the opposite. My favorite verse was Paul's desperate cry: "Why do I do the things I don't want to do and the things I don't want to do I do?" (Rom. 7:15–16, author's paraphrase).

By eighteen years of age I had tried every way except true surrender. I finally took all my pain fully to the cross of Jesus. I wept most Sundays as the band played, and as I came up to the front for prayer I felt what could only be described as the amazing, loving arms of a perfect Father. I finally found peace. I received God's forgiveness and felt so grateful for His death on the cross. His shed blood restored my life and healed my broken heart. Shortly afterward I went away on a Christian holiday, and someone showed me Revelation 3:16:

> *So, because you are lukewarm—neither hot nor*
> *cold—I am about to spit you out of my mouth.*

I hated seeing it like that. I decided that was it. I was 100 percent God's—the old was gone, and it was time for the new to come! I surrendered my whole heart to God and never looked back!

I knew, though, that when I eventually met my husband, there would be a whole catalog of sin and regret I would need to confess … and it made me feel nervous. I had been a very broken person, and I couldn't deny my history. A few years later, when Matt and I first got to know each other, he came to an event where I shared my testimony. Oops! That meant he'd hear about my past. I couldn't pretend I grew up on a farm, taught Sunday school from the age of seven, and lived the life of a nun! Instead he would hear the truth. *What if he rejected me? Had I blown it?* I started to fear that my past might ruin my future.

Eventually I talked with Matt about my fears, and he totally blew me away by saying so gently, "If Jesus sees you as pure, stunning, and spotless, how and why would I possibly see you any differently?" The past is just that—the *past*. When Matt sees me, he sees a beautiful new creation made whole and free by Jesus. I feel so loved and free.

The Enemy is always lying to us regarding the past, and my own little nagging shame from the past was awesomely extinguished when Matt spoke those words from God's heart over me. In that area I never again doubted God's acceptance. Fear and regret left the building!

Matt's proclamation of unconditional love and his desire to pursue a relationship with me blew my heart away—and caused me to rise up. I felt so secure. *Why was that? Was it because a boy was nice to me?* No, no, no! It was because Jesus used someone from whom I could receive truth to speak His incredible freedom to me. I heard the truth, and I accepted it—and never doubted again.

In this chapter I want to be your Matt Redman. I want you to hear the truth about the past and move into the fullness of God's amazing plans for your future!

God Recovers and Rescues Me

God demonstrates his own love for us in this: While we were still sinners, Christ died for us. (Rom. 5:8)

God saw us in our helpless, powerless, broken state and chose to rescue us and recover us. He sees our potential, not our problems. Jesus is like a master craftsman who finds an old chair abandoned in a garbage can. The chair is old, the paint is peeling, and the seat is torn apart. It is so damaged it cannot serve its original purpose. But the master craftsman sees no need for it to be thrown out—when he looks at the chair, he only sees what it can become! He sees that he can restore it back to its former glory. He lovingly, carefully, and painstakingly repairs the chair. It becomes more beautiful and even stronger than before.

You and I can be like that chair! In the hands of the master craftsman, what was damaged will be restored. Jesus takes what the world sees as useless, broken, and destroyed, and He carefully restores us. He rescues us from the trash and puts us back together into something even more glorious than the original.

Psalm 103:2–4 puts it like this: "Praise the Lord, O my soul, and forget not all his benefits—who forgives all your sins and heals all your diseases, who *redeems your life from the pit* and crowns you with love and compassion."

God sees the areas in our lives that need His master craftsmanship. He sees us in the middle of circumstances that we would do anything to hide away—He sees through our shame. Sometimes I am shocked by my deepest, darkest sinful thoughts. I can't believe who I am under the surface, but nothing shocks God. He is willing and able to go deep under the surface to mend us and bring peace and beauty from the ashes.

In John 4 we see a deeply moving encounter that Jesus had with a Samaritan woman who had everything to be ashamed of. Jesus entered Samaria—a country considered "unclean"—sat down at a well, and *began to talk to a woman*. It was extremely rare for a Jewish religious leader to speak with a woman in public. And not only did Jesus talk with her, He asked her for a drink, which according to religious custom of the day would have made Him ceremonially unclean. Jesus immediately defies massive religious preconceptions of whom God will sit with, who is and is not acceptable to God, and what is and is not clean. In the conversation that follows, Jesus freely offers her the gift of living water and eternal life: "Whoever drinks the water I give him will never thirst. Indeed, the water I give him will become in him a spring of water welling up to eternal life" (John 4:14).

Jesus knew all about this woman. In verse 18 Jesus simply says, "The fact is, you have had five husbands, and the man you now have is not your husband." But He still chose to come alongside her and drink with her. He wanted to have fellowship with her, and most of all He wanted to offer her eternal life. This encounter must have been unfathomable for this woman. She had lived a life of sin and shame in the eyes of society, and yet Jesus, the Son of

God, chose to come and sit next to her, draw water near to her, and drink with her. He even revealed to her His identity as the Messiah: "Then Jesus declared, 'I who speak to you am he'" (John 4:26).

Her history did not matter to Jesus, but her future did. The compassion, kindness, and love that Jesus showed during their conversation completely captivated her. Suddenly she felt loved, valued, and significant. No wonder she went throughout the town declaring, "Come, see a man who told me everything I ever did" (John 4:29). Rather than hide, she publicly rejoiced that Jesus knew everything because He took her sin and shame and left freedom and forgiveness in its place. He knew about her socially disgraceful past, and He met her in the middle of a difficult present to offer her an eternal future.

Insecurity can make it almost impossible to come into the presence of Jesus. But what we see here is that Jesus comes to her first, sits down, and drinks with this woman who has broken the law and breached what was morally acceptable. Jesus calls her just as He calls us. Even when we breach God's holy law and turn away from the path He chooses for us, *He waits for us*. He longs to fellowship with us and drink with us. God does not write us off because of our past. Jesus did not come for perfect people. He shed His perfect blood for every wrong choice and willful sin. He is calling and waiting at the figurative well to bring us back into relationship with Him. Where once you felt too guilty to approach Him, or where you have been terrified of the past being unveiled and dissected, know this: Jesus approaches *you*. He comes to you today, as you sit with your cup of tea or pour your glass of wine. He is there. We can run with confidence to His cross, to the place where Christ shed His blood for us: for the sins we committed, the offense we took, and the wrongs that were done to us. At that cross we find hope, healing, freedom, and forgiveness. *Woo hoo!*

God Restores Our Memories

"The former things will not be remembered, nor will they come to mind." (Isa. 65:17)

I watched a TV program recently called *The Dog Whisperer*. On the show, a dog trainer named Cesar Millan deals with all sorts of behavioral problems in dogs.

In one episode, Cesar went to help Ernesto, a smart, successful businessman in his forties. Ernesto had four children, all of whom loved dogs and wanted one as a pet. Yet Ernesto was utterly paralyzed by a fear of dogs. He, too, had once been like his children and loved dogs. Growing up in Mexico, most dogs Ernesto knew played independently in the streets, and he had no fear of them.

One day Ernesto and a group of friends were being silly and teasing one of the dogs—and *it snapped*. It turned on the group of children and started chasing them. Ernesto ran behind his friends toward his mother's house. The others all tumbled in and shut the door on him. He was left standing on the porch, and the last thing he remembered was the angry, snarling, vicious dog jumping for his throat. He woke up in the emergency room, and though he recovered from his horrific injuries, he was left deeply traumatized by the attack. By the time the Dog Whisperer came along thirty years later, a deep fear of dogs gripped Ernesto every day of his life. If he saw a dog or heard a distant bark, he relived the horror of that moment on the porch. Every day he feared a dog would attack him and lunge for his throat. His past utterly paralyzed his future. The intuitive and gifted dog trainer Cesar Millan spoke to Ernesto with a gentle authority.

"My friend," Cesar said, "what is holding you is the memory, but the incident is gone. You are allowing that memory to live on with you every single day. We have to break the power of the memory and allow you to live in the freedom. It is over!"

Cesar took Ernesto to a rehabilitation center for wayward dogs. He opened the door to the dogs' exercise area, and there before Ernesto were around fifty dogs.

Ernesto was terrified, but again Cesar spoke with gentle authority and brought a truth that freed this poor wounded man from his thirty-year prison.

"The dog who attacked you is dead," Cesar said. "You are not going to be attacked." In other words, forget the past and live in the present.

In that moment, as Ernesto faced his fear and became a free man, completely transformed and released, and he went and petted the dogs and walked alongside them without fear.

Many of us are like Ernesto. Memories of past events, traumas, and mistakes live on in our minds and affect how we react to our circumstances today. It may not be a fear of dogs; it may be something more horrific—but a memory can hold you captive, influencing your thinking and the decisions you make.

Noah Luca

Months before I got pregnant with our second son, Noah, I felt God wake me up in the middle of the night and say, "You are going to have a son, and he will be called Noah Luca ... but he will be known as *Luca*." When I looked up *Luca,* I found that the name meant "a bringer of light." *Amazing.* Sure enough I soon delivered a boy, and we called him Noah Luca. Just as the agony of my labor was coming to an end and Noah was about to be born, Matt interrupted me to draw my attention to a rainbow outside. I was *so* unimpressed. Who cares about a stupid, floaty rainbow when I am in excruciating pain?

Our beautiful boy came out but he did not make the sweet, gurgly noise that Maisey-Ella had made two years before. Instead he emerged gasping and groaning and blue. They laid Noah on my chest, and he gasped deeper and deeper. A bell rang; the doctors ran in and whisked him away. I thought he'd come back a moment later, but he did not return to our room. What seemed like hours passed, and we had no idea what was going on. They wheeled me into an elevator where I sat beside a lady holding her baby boy in her arms. I sobbed for my baby.

In the intensive care unit I saw a baby in a box, with a machine breathing for him and with tubes everywhere. I looked up and saw on the board written in red letters: "Baby Boy Redman. CRITICAL."

I started to cry. *What was happening to our boy? Was he going to die?*

Days went by, and still we could not hold our son. Our precious friend and pastor, Mike Pilavachi (Noah's godfather), was visiting when the doctor interrupted and asked to see Matt and me. Mike left the room, and the doctor sat us down and told us that Noah was in an even more critical state, and the next twenty-four hours would determine whether or not he would survive. It was the worst moment of my life.

Immediately Mike arranged for people all over the world to pray. We clung to God and prayed for Noah to live. The next day the miraculous occurred, and twenty-four hours after that Noah was lying in an open incubator breathing by himself. God rescued him and restored his breath!

A week later we brought our boy home, and yet I felt like I could not celebrate. I felt numb. Matt would ask me, "Why are you low? Noah is alive!"

But I still held onto the trauma and the memory of his fight for life. I kept reliving the grief of him being taken, the fear of him dying, and the agony of leaving our tiny baby on a breathing machine in the hospital while we slept at home.

I realized past events held me, and through prayer I took all the memories, flashbacks, and grief to the cross of Jesus. God freed me to live in the here and now and properly celebrate our amazing God and His incredible gift to us: Noah Luca. Instead of saying, "He nearly died," I was able to say, "He is alive and well."

It was then I laughed and remembered the rainbow Matt had shown me. At the time it had seemed irrelevant, a rude interruption.

However, as we look back now, it was a glorious sign to Matt and me of God's promise to us before our son's conception that we would have a son called *Noah* who would live to be a bringer of light. I believe that and celebrate that with my whole heart. In the Bible God sent a rainbow to Noah as a sign of His promise. He had foretold a flood, but the rainbow signified His goodness and the end of the heavy rains. A new day would dawn, and the sun would start to shine and dry up the mess.

It was over.

I want to encourage you in the midst of whatever painful memories may hold you or rob you: *God is calling you to look up and see the rainbow.* It might seem insensitive or frustrating to think outside of or above your pain, but that rainbow is an incredible reminder for you that God is good, a new day is coming, eventually the rain will stop, and beauty and promise will reign over your life!

Song of Solomon 2:11–12 says, "See! The winter is past; the rains are over and gone. Flowers appear on the earth, the season of singing has come." Grieve, mourn, heal, and receive the amazing power of prayer. All those things are healthy and right. Lean on Jesus and allow Him to free you from the memories, the trauma, or the regret. When we hand over our questions, our struggles, and our bad memories to Jesus, they are gone, buried, removed, and separated from us *forever.*

Psalm 103:1–2 says, "Praise the LORD, O my soul; all my inmost being, praise his holy name. Praise the LORD, O my soul, and forget not all his benefits."

As we praise, we remind ourselves—our inmost being, our hearts, minds, and memories—that the Lord forgave us our past, took our life out of the mess we made of it, restored us to the glory we were created for, and crowned us with love and compassion. When we remember this, how can we spend any time worrying about the past?

The Woman Caught in Adultery

In John chapter 8, we read about a woman who has been caught in adultery. This means she was found having adulterous sex, so she was literally caught in the act. As if this was not shameful enough, men dragged her out in front of her entire community and told her how shameful and disgusting she was. I wonder if deep down this woman felt loved, had a purpose, or knew God's heart of love and compassion for her. *Probably not.* This woman's pain caused her to become broken and to feel worthless. She may already have felt disgusting and ashamed of herself. Then she was caught in the act, and the stones came out. She may have felt that she deserved to die as her outraged accusers looked at her in disgust. Are we supposed to feel sorry for this filthy harlot? *Totally.* Jesus knows all and forgives all. Right there in the midst of an attempted murder scene, the God of mercy stepped in. This is the same God of mercy who steps in for us.

While accusing voices humiliated this woman, Jesus directly challenged *the accusers*: "If any one of you is without sin, let him be the first to throw a stone at her" (John 8:7). The phrase *without sin* is quite general and means "without any sin," *not* "without this particular sin." When we mess up, there is always a line of people trying to make us feel terrible and tell us how we have failed. But we need to remember mercy. Jesus didn't condone sin … but He showed mercy.

When we are going through desperate, difficult times, the hardest thing can be hearing the voices of condemnation, rejection, and shame from others. The Enemy—the accuser of our brothers—loves to use people to kick us in the stomach when we're down. The Enemy loves to use our sin to condemn us rather than allow us to hear the conviction of the Holy Spirit. Here in John 8 we see an angry religious community surrounding this woman like a pack of wolves baying for condemnation and punishment.

Yet Jesus turns their anger and thirst for vengeance back on themselves. As each one remembers how he or she, too, has sinned—the older members among them walk away first—Jesus and the woman are left alone. Jesus silences the condemning voices and commands them to leave. In His presence it becomes clear that *all* have sinned and fallen short. Only Jesus is capable of judging properly. Now Jesus is able to deal with this broken, fallen woman. Listen to the kindness in His voice as He says in John 8:10–11,

> *"Woman, where are they? Has no one condemned you?"*
> *"No one, sir," she said.*
> *"Then neither do I condemn you," Jesus declared.*

The world, the Enemy, and, sadly, other *religious* people are often so quick to condemn and get the stones out. But it is not Jesus who condemns. Rather, He says, "Go now, and leave your life of sin" (John 8:11).

Many of us are all too familiar with stories of friends who have fallen from great heights, amazing callings, and lives of blessing after they were led into temptation and sin. Maybe you are one of those people. Maybe you have been caught in adultery and now hear the loud voices of the church, your family, and others condemning you and telling you how awful you are.

Jesus does not condemn you, but He does speak clearly to the situation. Jesus says, "Go now, and leave your life of sin." Stop what you are doing, and return to Jesus. Jesus is your home. So come home! Don't let those voices of condemnation and judgment prevent you from hearing truth and receiving forgiveness. Don't stop yourself from coming to Jesus, repenting with all your heart, and turning from your sin and back to your life with Christ. *Turn around* now, and hear the voice of Jesus calling you home. Revelation 2:5 says,

> *Remember the height from which you have*
> *fallen! Repent and do the things you did at first.*

Don't just feel sorrow and regret—hear the kindness and urgency in God's voice as He says, "Go now, and leave your life of sin."

Maybe you have seen others fall away. Maybe you recognize, with horror, your voice in the crowd, calling for punishment and judgment on your brother or sister. In Luke 6:37–38, Jesus says, "Do not judge, and you will not be judged. Do not condemn, and you will not be condemned. Forgive, and you will be forgiven.… For with the measure you use, it will be measured to you."

Yes, it is terrible when a brother or sister falls from a blessed life of calling. It is terrible because that fall is the plan of the Enemy to kill and steal and destroy, not the plan of your loving heavenly Father, which is to bless, prosper, and give hope and a future. When we hear of such things and watch our friends fall painfully into sin and despair, let's gently call them back to repentance, not tell them how dreadful they are. When someone hurts you or is inconsiderate, let's not stand in judgment and condemnation. It is for Jesus alone to judge. Jesus calls us to love one another. Let's not be yet another voice of accusation or condemnation. Be the voice of love and forgiveness, urging others to repent and return to Jesus.

If you are living in the past, in rejection, in failure, in shame, or in sorrow, I encourage you—*choose Jesus.*

Deuteronomy 30:19–20 says:

> *"This day I call heaven and earth as witnesses against you that I have set before you life and death, blessings and curses. Now choose life, so that you and your children may live and that you may love the LORD your God, listen to his voice, and hold fast to him. For the LORD is your life, and he will give you many years in the land he swore to give to your fathers, Abraham, Isaac and Jacob."*

I know that Jesus called every one of us. You have a choice. *Your voice or His voice. Your way or His way.* I implore you—choose His way, the way of abundant life.

Chapter Three

GOD SHAPES MY CHARACTER

The youngest of eight brothers, David was charged with the seemingly mundane responsibility of watching over the family sheep. This was a job of both extreme danger and utter boredom. He had to find grass and water in a dry, stony land and protect the sheep from bad weather and predators. Even though the job was usually monotonous, David was a "shepherd of honor and courage," fighting bears and lions to protect his father's sheep. During times of quiet he made the most of the mundane, and as he sat in the field he was content, writing songs of worship and singing to his Maker. He was peaceful and grateful in that place.

If it had been me, I wonder if I would have sat there so nicely. I think I would have grumbled at the unenviable task of hanging with sheep all day and all night! So why did he not fume and whine about his misfortune of being the youngest and therefore qualifying for the lowliest position in the family?

He did not burn with selfish ambition or struggle with resentment at his lonely and often arduous job because his character was being molded and shaped by heaven. He glorified God where others might have mumbled and questioned, and as David carried out his life in this way, his service and humility were like worship, and he caught the attention of God. Out of a servant's heart and godly contentment a shepherd boy was promoted to king. Even in his lowly position he genuinely loved his sheep, and as he worked obediently and humbly, God shaped his character so that one day he could shepherd God's people.

The early life of David is a sharpening story from which we can learn so much. If you want to walk in the plans God has for you, *submit to Him shaping your character!*

On reflection, David wasn't just learning skills in a field at night when it was hard and no one was watching but God—rather, God was shaping his character. So we can be encouraged! When life seems to be dull and meaningless, and no human words of affirmation or recognition are ringing in our ears, let's capture some of David's attitude and say yes to the unseen makeover that can take place within!

Developing a Beautiful Character

Your beauty should not come from outward adornment, such as braided hair and the wearing of gold jewelry and fine clothes. Instead, it should be that of your inner self, the unfading beauty of a gentle and quiet spirit, which is of great worth in God's sight. (1 Peter 3:3–4)

Peter knew that beauty is far more than skin deep. The kind of dress he talks about in 1 Peter 3 seems irrelevant and stuffy for us today. But as we look at why he guided women to avoid this type of headwear, we see that women wore those items to allure and seduce others in a sexual manner—therefore these things were considered a sign of bad character. The folding of the hair was a specific, ornate, and extravagant custom. Hairstyles often overflowed with ringlets, plaits, or were covered with flowers. Traditionally women wore head coverings as sign of reverence and modesty, so these ornate plaits were brazen displays of rebellion designed to ensnare a man.

Similarly, the gold jewelry Peter talks about was not simply a few necklaces and rings. These women wore gold crowns on their heads! This tradition began after the destruction of the temple, and Jewish women would wear a gold crown in memory of Jerusalem on the Sabbath. They were originally worn as a sign of reverence in the temple, but women began to wear something sacred for everyday use—dressing inappropriately for the attention and possible entrapment of men.

So as we read 1 Peter and examine his words closely—yes, the first thing Peter says is *dress appropriately!* The second thing he says is that the things you think make you beautiful are not truly beautiful at all. Beauty comes from the character and the heart within. So every morning when we think about what we are going to wear, let's check our motives. Check our hearts. Are we putting on a cleavage-enhancing top today? Do we need to share our most up-front parts with the world? Peter says be discreet and modest; let your *inner* qualities shine and speak for you, not items of clothing or full-frontal styling that's clearly for someone else's benefit! These verses sharpen me to be responsible in the way I dress and to examine my motives.

But also, God says the inner you is precious and worth beautifying for His glory!

While all the magazines say to us, *exhaust your savings and focus your time chasing after clothes, jewelry, and the latest hairdo in an effort to attain outward beauty and acceptance,* Peter says, *spend your time chasing after the things that are beautiful and precious to God.*

So, let's look at how to work on our character, so that our inner selves will truly glow. These pious women of old that Peter talks about grasped that: "The LORD does not look at the things man looks at. Man looks at the outward appearance, but the LORD looks at the heart" (1 Sam. 16:7). God chooses and prioritizes a beautiful heart. He looks inside, beyond the surface, and values what is inside of you.

I recently underwent the most horrible facial I have ever experienced. It was called the "Remedy Signature Facial," which sounded great, and I pretended to know what the beautician was talking about, nodding along when she asked me if I was familiar with the "microdermabrasion process."

Well, I soon realized I was not familiar with the process!

I can only describe it as like a thousand razors grating over your skin, with glass on the end of each one. This process extracts the dead skin and the impurities, *and it is horrible.* After the agony, the woman "oxygenates" your face and puts some lovely things on your skin. It was the most aggressive beauty treatment I have ever experienced in my life.

But when I looked in the mirror afterward, I didn't look wounded or scarred; my face looked alive and fresh, because the treatment had gone below the surface! There's a spiritual method that is not too dissimilar from microdermabrasion that can give us a fantastic result—*quickly.*

The first part is to go under the microscope and remove the dead rubbish. We need to start by examining the hidden person of the heart, the person we are when no one is around. The part of us that will reach heaven and be perfect one day—but right now it's a glorious work in progress! The prayer of Psalm 139:23–24 helps us begin this process as we say, "Search me, O God, and know my heart; test me and know my anxious thoughts. See if there is any offensive way in me, and lead me in the way everlasting."

When we are looking for "offensive ways," we're not talking about "moments"—times when we are really stressed and stretched and just lose it. No, we're talking about areas of consistent bad character in our lives.

It might be swearing. It might be not being able to forgive. It might be having a quick temper, being cruel, or gossiping. The beautifying process opens my eyes so God can show me who I really am. It gives me the space to repent and throw myself on the mercy of God so I can say: "Help God! She's back! That woman I don't want to be—anxious and wrought up, lashing out at the people I love! I want to be gentle and full of peace! I want to be able to hold my tongue. I want peace in the midst of the storm."

Then we take those areas of bad character to the cross. Jesus forgives them, extracts that moment and that sin. He says, "Come to Me, consistently, every day. Just as you wash your face and brush your teeth every morning, come to Me every day of your life, and then we can get into the oxygenating, moisturizing phase where all the nourishing good stuff goes in."

In place of a stressful, anxious heart, God wants to give you a peaceful, quiet spirit. I never thought I could have this. If you're naturally bubbly, loud, and exuberant, it can be easy to think that being meek and having a quiet spirit means you will have to be quiet and never speak. But we're not talking about crushing the personality that God has given you. *No!* We need every type of person God has made. But the outer casing has within it a character of quietness and meekness that doesn't butt in or push itself to the front or try to be the center of attention. Those that possess this gentle quiet spirit …

- … are not easily provoked to anger
- … patiently bear and put up with injuries
- … carry themselves affably and courteously unto all
- … believe the best of others
- … do not envy the gifts and graces of others
- … are willing to be instructed by the meanest saint (to suffer unjustly)

These people quietly submit to the will of God, and they subscribe all that they have to the free grace of God.

Don't you want to have that as the core of who you are? Women with these characteristics are amazing in the middle of a crisis. They are amazing present helpers in the homes of the hurting. They are amazing ambassadors on the streets for Jesus.

This nature is everything that our lovely Jesus is. Running after Him is putting the worship album on in the car and putting Him first as you start your day, living for Him and chasing Him, running *first* to the One who made us and can shape us and transform us, and acknowledging that we're here on this planet for *Him!*

It's about making the commitment to find a moment to open your Bible—and there He provides you with a precious treasure to get you through the day; you're pressing in, absorbing, and releasing His Word and nature into your heart and life. You are beautifying your character.

As we travel this journey of faith we keep examining ourselves and checking our character so that we can be "renewed day by day" (2 Cor. 4:16). Every day as we absorb more of Jesus we will become more beautiful, until finally we are made perfect with Him in heaven. Hooray!

Humility

He guides the humble in what is right and teaches them his way.
(Ps. 25:9)

Recently, I was watching the UK version of *The Apprentice*. It is often quite uncomfortable watching the candidates' brutal fight for survival. In the boardroom each week, as many potential employees are on the cusp of ejection, some will say and do anything to discredit their colleagues to maintain their chances of staying in another week. Of course, the show is an exaggeration of office life, but it still deeply illuminates each candidate's ambition and pride. Yasmina, the winner of *The Apprentice* UK 2009 says of herself, "I'm extremely ruthless. I will go out of my way to obtain whatever

I can get. I think being successful is more important than being popular."

And Yasmina was one of the nicer ones!

We are not to live like candidates on *The Apprentice,* tearing one another down and treading over others to get to the top. Instead, the Bible says, "Don't push your way to the front; don't sweet-talk your way to the top. Put yourself aside, and help others get ahead" (Phil. 2:3 MSG).

Even Sir Alan Sugar (the Donald Trump of the UK) said to his contestants: "Personality opens the door. Character keeps it open." If character is important to a tough businessman like Sir Alan, how much more important is it to God?

Part of the godly character we are called to develop is humility. Proverbs 15:33 says, "The fear of the LORD teaches a man wisdom, and humility comes before honor." So, all us eager apprentices, here's an amazing tip from the top! Humble yourself before the Lord's mighty hand, and He will lift you up!

I once heard a pastor of a huge and thriving church say that all of the staff positions were selected from the volunteers who served faithfully week in, week out for no pay simply because they loved God and wanted to build His church. The ones who, like David, did an amazing job with a humble heart while no one was watching or rewarding them. This pastor sent an awesome message out to his church: Character is more important than experience or qualifications. This would be a little odd and weak in the eyes of the world. But God's Word says this: "God chose the foolish things of the world to shame the wise; God chose the weak things of the world to shame the strong" (1 Cor. 1:27).

This may seem a weak and senseless idea, but God has ordained that His church be built on the things the world considers weakness, not on that which appears to be strong. He does this to force us to trust in His strength and wisdom, not our own. This way we can't boast in our own abilities. That's what humility is—acknowledging that God's ways, plans, and purposes are greater than anything we could ever dream of or achieve on our own … and being awestruck that He chose to use us.

Submitting to God

"If anyone would come after me, he must deny himself and take up his cross and follow me." (Matt. 16:24)

The Lord sees not only who and what you are right now, but also what you can become. Hooray and phew! He can use us just as we are, but He will also increase our strength according to our needs.

When God asked Moses to go to Pharaoh and demand he release the Israelites, Moses' response is remarkably human: "O Lord, … I am slow of speech and tongue … O Lord, please send someone else to do it" (Ex. 4:10, 13). Moses had a terrible stutter and a tendency to try to squirm out of his calling and responsibility! God is patient with us as He works in and through us, and the man who asked God to send someone else became one of Israel's greatest leaders. In contrast, we see Isaiah, in chapter 6, wholeheartedly offering himself before the Lord: "Here am I. Send me!" (v. 8). As we lay our lives down before Jesus, He is able to pick us up and use us for His purposes.

However, that is not always an easy thing to do, nor does it always have the consequences that we would intend for our lives.

When I was young I wanted to work in TV. While at college I saw an ad for a job as an assistant at a production company. I was so excited and saw this as the ticket to my dream! I went to the interview and prayed continually, *Lord, please open the door if it is You, and shut it if not.* My flesh wanted that job so much, but as I prayed for God's will to be done I felt a quiet trust. I didn't get that job, and although I stamped my foot for five minutes, I can see by praying and trusting God He allowed the wrong doors to close and the right doors to fling wide open.

As David spent years wrestling bears and sitting in the fields, God worked on his behalf and began setting things in place. All David had to do was get up when his name was called, and he was anointed king! *How incredible!* This encourages me when I am sitting still and enduring things that are mundane or frustrating. That's when I remember that if I am humble and obedient, content and faithful, what might feel like disappointment is actually an opportunity for future hope. If we trust God in the lonely fields, we know He will open amazing doors.

Trusting God with the Desires of Your Heart

When we talk about *submitting* to the will of God, we raise serious issues of trust. It is entirely countercultural to submit to anyone or anything.

Frank Sinatra's best-selling hymn to himself—"My Way"— neatly sums up today's values and priorities:

I planned each charted course,

each careful step along the byway,

and more, much more than this,

I did it my way.[1]

Laying down our lives, then, is not natural to the flesh! We long to plan our own destiny, be masters of, if not the universe, then at least our own realm! Yet God calls us to lay down our lives, give it all up, and humbly follow Him. God showed Himself trustworthy when He came down from heaven and became man, then bled and died for us on the cross so that we could enter into an eternal relationship with Him. Again and again He calls us to trust Him—to trust that He is good, that He has the best planned for us. Trust is similar to faith in that we trust what we know, not what we feel or maybe even see. When we trust God, we let go of our expectations for our lives, of our desire to control events and people and ourselves, and we let God sit in the driver's seat. In the Bible, trusting God is key to seeing His plans for our lives unfold as we see in Psalm 37:3–6:

> *Trust in the LORD and do good;*
> *dwell in the land and enjoy safe pasture.*

> *Delight yourself in the LORD*
> *and he will give you the desires of your*
> *heart.*

> *Commit your way to the LORD;*
> *trust in him and he will do this:*

He will make your righteousness shine like the
dawn,
    the justice of your cause like the noonday
sun.

What is amazing is that as we put our trust in God, He is able to work in our lives for His glory. When we stop striving and trying to make it all happen by ourselves, He is able to step in and work out the plans He has for us. God knows us—He made us—and He sees the desires of our hearts. Sometimes we can be afraid of those desires. We can be fearful of admitting to ourselves what they actually are, in case they never happen and we end up disappointed. God sees the dreams of our hearts sometimes without us even telling Him. There are things I dreamed of that God has fulfilled over and above my wildest hopes, and there are dreams and desires I've presented and requested, and the answer seems to be, for now and maybe forever, a *no*. We have to trust Him and love Him enough to be grateful for each gift of grace, and be patient and humble when we wait. He wants us to commit each day, decision, and thought to Him. Then He can use us in the most unique way for the kingdom and for His glory, in a way that we would never have been able to make happen ourselves.

God Directs Our Paths

Trust in the LORD *with all your heart and lean not on your own understanding; in all your ways acknowledge him, and he will make your paths straight. (Prov. 3:5–6)*

When we acknowledge God in all our ways, we listen to His words, obey His commands, and value His thoughts over and above our own. We submit our desires to Him and deliberately choose to walk in His ways. Then as the Lord sees our choices, how we choose to live, and our choice to honor Him in all we do, He will make our paths straight and bless us. The Bible is clear that the Lord directs us in His path if we trust Him and are open to His direction. This might surprise you, but God is better at working out our lives than we are! He knows what we need, He knows that we are weak and frail, but He longs to bless us, in the appointed time, in His perfect way. I have found over the years that sometimes a *no* is as good for my soul as a *yes*.

A *no* forces me to increase my trust. When I am seeking Him for abundance, sometimes on reflection it seems His *no* was an amazing way to increase my dependence. Trusting God does not mean simply waiting around passively for a master plan to fall into our laps. Jesus clearly teaches us that we are to pray about everything we need, and today that may well have as much to do with decisions and careers as our daily bread. Matthew 7:8–11 says this:

> *"For everyone who asks receives; he who seeks finds; and to him who knocks, the door will be opened. Which of you, if his son asks for bread, will give him a stone? Or if he asks for a fish, will give him a snake? If you, then, though you are evil, know how to give good gifts to your children, how much more will your Father in heaven give good gifts to those who ask him!"*

Jesus paints for us a vivid picture of God's goodness as a loving, caring father. God is *good* and "is able to do immeasurably more than all we ask or imagine" (Eph. 3:20). So dream about what you would like to see the Lord do in your life. Don't be afraid of the desires of your heart—listen to them and ask God for them. Confidently present your prayers and petitions before the Father. Then be like David. Serve with all eyes on the job with contentment, and quietly trust in Him, only looking up from the field to worship.

God Has a Plan for You

"For I know the plans I have for you," declares the LORD, *"plans to prosper you and not to harm you, plans to give you hope and a future. Then you will call upon me and come and pray to me, and I will listen to you. You will seek me and find me when you seek me with all your heart." (Jer. 29:11–13)*

God's plan for each and every one of us is amazing. Not boring, dull, or drab, but an explosive plan that could cause us and those around us to flourish and grow. God tailor-makes plans for each of us. As Jeremiah says, His plans contain hope and promises of a future. They are by their very nature good, not bad. There will surely be hardships along the way, but His plans and His will turn evil to good, and trials and broken hopes will be restored through Jesus. It means we can be safe and have hope for tomorrow.

However, these plans are not just wheeled out on a trolley and delivered to our doorstep! Jeremiah 29:13 shows us that to obtain this "hope and future," God wants to work in our lives, not forcing us to strive or pretend to be good girls to get in His good books. Rather He wants us to lay down our own plans and dreams first and submit to Him in humility and trust. So often I would quote this verse to myself and to others and feel confident everything I ever wished for would be mine because God said so! For years I did not understand the significance of the next part of the verse. Yes, *oh yes*—God does have great things for us! All can receive Jesus, but all must choose Him first. The same goes for His plans for us. He does not act without us being willing and playing our part. Seeking God with all our hearts is the prerequisite to finding Him. So how do we go about doing this in our everyday lives?

God Is the Opener of Doors

Matthew 7:8 says that "to him who knocks, the door will be opened." We are able to knock on God's door with confidence, knowing that He will welcome us in. A door may also represent an opportunity or a new direction God has planned for us. In Revelation 3:8, Jesus says, "I know your deeds. See, I have placed before you an open door that no one can shut."

God makes everything beautiful in His perfect time. Put your faith and trust in God, and ask Him to shut the wrong doors and open the right ones. When we let God take control, we allow Him to work miracles of great joy and power in our lives.

When the things we want and dream about do not come to pass, we must choose to fight against becoming bitter or angry, and instead deliberately lay all our plans before the Lord. Our walk is to be God-centered, not me-centered. May your daily aim be to make the most of every opportunity to be faithful and obedient, to seek His face and His path in your life, and to resist the temptation to make things happen yourself.

God Graciously Blesses Us

"But blessed is the man who trusts in the LORD,
  whose confidence is in him.
He will be like a tree planted by the water
  that sends out its roots by the stream.
  It does not fear when heat comes;
  its leaves are always green.
  It has no worries in a year of drought
  and never fails to bear fruit." (*Jer. 17:7–8*)

This verse from Jeremiah brings incredible peace and comfort. It promises that as we shift our trust to the Lord, God will bless us with a confidence that He will provide all that we need. Our trust and confidence in Him will be richly rewarded as we soak up His presence and His words of truth in our lives. In 1 Chronicles 17:16–17 we hear the amazement and gratitude of David at the lavish outpouring of blessing and favor God has bestowed upon him: "Who am I, O LORD God, and what is my family, that you have brought me this far? And as if this were not enough in your sight, O God, you have spoken about the future of the house of your servant." He continues in verses 25 and 26: "You, my God, have revealed to your servant that you will build a house for him. So your servant has found courage to pray to you. O LORD, you are God! You have promised these good things to your servant."

What amazing grace! David wasn't perfect, not by any means. In worldly terms he did not deserve all that God gave him—he could never have worked to earn such lavish blessing—but God in His grace chose to give it to David freely.

David was faithful, trusting, obedient, patient, humble, and content in all circumstances. This pleased God immensely, because David's attitude and his daily life choices honored God. As you honor God in your life and develop a godly character, you grow in trust, submission, and humility, and God will bless you, lead you, and guide you. A life dedicated to Him will be richly rewarding and an incredible adventure. I am so excited to watch as we continue to trust and see His beautiful plans for us unfold!

Chapter Four

God Sees My Choices

Free will is an amazing gift, but also an awesome responsibility. Each choice we make has consequences for our lives.

God sees how we choose to live, what we choose to honor and value in our lives, and how we rank Him in the decisions that we make. If we choose to seek and place God first, He promises us we will find Him.

Running Your Race

Therefore, since we are surrounded by such a great cloud of witnesses, let us throw off everything that hinders and the sin that so easily entangles, and let us run with perseverance the race marked out for us. Let us fix our eyes on Jesus, the author and perfecter of our faith, who for the joy set before him endured the cross, scorning its shame, and sat down at the right hand of the throne of God. (Heb. 12:1–2)

For fitness (not fun), I regularly go spinning. This is an exercise class that involves sitting on a stationary bike and peddling your butt

off for up to an hour while an instructor rides in front and continually makes the process tougher.

I first tried spinning a few years ago, and I absolutely *loathed*
it. In the sparse gym there was nothing to keep me motivated, and
as all the fluorescent lights shone down in the room each week, I
could clearly be seen as the worst in the group! However, when we
moved to America I joined a new gym. At my first spinning class I
was delighted to see that the lights dimmed the minute we started
peddling, which meant that each rider in the room was not aware of
anyone else's race. So we just focused hard on our own. Also as we
cycled, a projector descended and a very motivating scene began to
unfold. For sixty minutes, as we pedaled through imaginary hills and
rough terrain, we watched another race taking place and being won.
It was the ultimate race between professional cyclists—the Tour de
France.

The projector showed the competitors ascending the harshest of hills with steely determination, and as they raced along the
course, a throng of enthusiastic supporters cheered them on. As
we watched them race, our own instructor, positioned at the front,
encouraged us on over the loud speaker. She intuitively prepared us
for the steep hills and motivated us when we struggled and began
to lose momentum.

In Hebrews 12 we read a similar scene. A runner enters the
Olympic stadium and begins his race. *The race of faith*. All the time
this runner has the surrounding encouragement of the heroes of the
faith and the image of Jesus ahead of him to spur him on; Jesus is his
instructor and the One who endured, overcame the Enemy, finished
His race, and won the prize in heaven.

However, unlike the Tour de France, this race of faith is more of a contest than a competition. The runner in Hebrews is not competing against others, but he chooses to run, focused on Jesus, straining to achieve all God has for him and not giving up in the process. The Greek word for race is *agona*—which means a contest or struggle. The race of faith is not a church-against-church, believer-against-believer contest. The Bible says our *agona* is not against flesh and blood but against the Enemy. So throughout this race the runners compete with the Enemy, who is continually trying to throw them off course. The most successful way to defeat him is to look toward Jesus. As we read the Bible, listen to teaching, feed our souls, and worship in spirit and truth, we choose to run as the writer of Hebrews instructs. Those choices are like liquid fuel that give us the tools we need in our race to resist the lies, temptations, and distractions of the Enemy.

So in Hebrews 12 as the writer tells each saint to "run the race marked out for you," he reiterates our uniqueness. Not only are we each one-of-a-kind, but we also have an individually designed course to run. It conjures up images of lanes on a track and we each have our own. *I love that!* The course and the contents of your race will be different from your best friend's race or the one the girl next door to you is running. God has crafted plans and purposes that only you can fulfill, a path that only you can take, and a race that you alone run. I feel so privileged and validated that no one else can do the job He has for me!

Sometimes we can get so distracted by other people's gifts, favors, or callings that we spend too much time wishing we were running their race, and we stop running ours altogether. The

result is that we lose the joy of the adventure that God has for
each of us.

Throw Off Everything that Hinders

In order to win our *agona*, the writer gives us some more great
running tips. In Hebrews 12:1 it states clearly: "Let us throw off
everything that hinders and the sin that so easily entangles, and let
us run with perseverance the race marked out for us."

A hindrance is any kind of heavy weight. Stop to think right
now, *what are the things weighing me down or discouraging me in my
faith today?* It could be a relationship, a negative thought pattern, the
need to forgive someone, or anything that slows you down, weighs
on you, and hinders your performance and your potential. The
writer is calling out to you and me to make the choice to "strip off
every weight that slows you down" (Heb. 12:1, author's paraphrase).

In the time of the letter to the Hebrews, athletes would compete
in Olympic-style races wearing nothing but loincloths. By removing
layers of unwanted clothing they were able to run as fast as possible
without distraction or irritation.

Anything that weighs heavily on us spiritually can tempt us to
lose heart, and in some instances, when the weight is heavy, to lose
faith completely. I want to run to Jesus, to be all He has called me
to be, to overcome everything His grace says I can overcome, and to
push through the painful part of my race to the other side: to victory,
to Jesus, to truth, and to the completion of all He set out for me to
do. We mustn't let the Enemy's lies permeate our flesh and have free
reign on our thinking. Run through the doubt, the disappointment,

and the fear. Don't let anything fester into sin. That sin will so easily entangle you. Whenever negative thoughts threaten to drag us down and overwhelm us, we must choose to replace them with the truth of God. In John 8:31–32, Jesus says, "If you hold to my teaching, you are really my disciples. Then you will know the truth, and the truth will set you free."

One year we returned to the UK for a Christmas visit. We have five children now, but during this particular trip we had four children, and the youngest was just six weeks old. The adult-to-child ratio was not ideal, and the age ranges were challenging! In order to make the journey as easy as possible I decided we should pack only hand luggage. On the way there, my plan worked really well, and we got through passport control quickly, feeling rather pleased with ourselves.

On the return journey, it was a different story.

We all had much more luggage, because of all the Christmas presents we had received and all the extras we'd bought. Matt and I each now had a rucksack as well as a carry-on suitcase, plus a baby, a toddler, and the older two. Rocco got the best seat of all: the stroller. I pushed him and carried six-week-old Jackson in a sling. As I had the babies, Matt divided the remaining bags between him and the older two kids. As we got off the plane we turned the corner and saw the longest line I have ever seen at immigration! We got ourselves in line, and poor Matt had to endure moving forward every fifteen seconds with all the carry-on handbags as the children complained of exhaustion every few steps. Rocco fussed constantly, and poor sweet Jackson cried as he overheated against my chest (did I mention I was wearing three layers, a winter coat, and holding the baby?).

It was freezing outside, so we'd layered up, but the kind people in the airport had turned the heating up to keep everyone snug. And there was no way we could take our coats off as we were already carrying so much.

So it was official: My space-time-saving idea had well and truly bitten me on the butt. We stood in that line for nearly *two hours*. Just to add to my self-inflicted misery, I had chosen to wear my stiletto boots, as they were too big to fit into my carry-on bag. I had self-sabotaged my journey. I was inappropriately dressed for the situation, and as the line moved toward the finish I could barely stand.

When we finally got to the booth I totally lost it! Normally the immigration officers are pretty scary, but I know for sure I scared this guy!

I started telling him about our ordeal and declared my disgust at the circumstances—then to top it off I insisted somewhat loudly: "Get me a wheelchair—I'm going to pass out!"

Matt and the children laughed!

When we finally arrived home and the children were safely tucked in bed, I took off all my cumbersome layers, peeled off my evil stiletto boots, and fell into bed defeated.

Looking at Hebrews 12 the next day, my arduous airport experience reminded me of how I have sometimes lived as a Christian. I was so burdened in that line that I struggled to take even a few steps and did not feel at all victorious as I reached the end.

Similarly, there have been times in my Christian life when I have been so weighed down with hurt and sin that I felt like giving up. As I tried to run ahead and be all God called me to be, I instead struggled on tired and ashamed. It seemed so cruel that nobody came to help us in that line in Atlanta. No one turned down the heat or removed my painful boots. And why would they? The amazing news is, as Christians on the journey of life, when we are weary and burdened in our race we can call on the name of Jesus—and as the writer of Hebrews urges, "Throw off everything that hinders." That night as I finally threw off my boots I felt such release.

How many of us waste years of our race being held back unnecessarily? Let's address these things quickly and carry on as it says in 1 Peter: "Cast all your anxiety on him because he cares for you" (1 Peter 5:7). Metaphorically speaking, strip down to your undies like the Olympic athletes of Rome. This is the one time it's good to keep it skimpy!

Some of you are trying to run your race of faith in your heels, carrying big suitcases and covered in bags. It's time to get free! Draw a line, forgive, move on, breathe truth, accept the past, and whatever your hindrance is, throw it off today! Live in the truth. Consider Jesus. Think about Him. Fix your eyes upon Jesus, who carried His cross all the way to the finish line. Look full in His wonderful face.

God asks us to make a clear mental choice to unburden ourselves.

Sometimes we are so caught up in our feelings and our misfortunes, we need to put them aside and as the Bible says "consider Him … so that you will not grow weary and lose heart" (Heb. 12:3).

As we look up and consider Jesus, we also have a great cloud of witnesses—all the mighty men and women of God spoken of in Hebrews 11 who lived lives of faith and obedience—to encourage us and spur us on. Just as I watched my spinning video and felt encouraged by enthusiastic supporters cheering and waving banners, so we have men and women of incredible faith like Abraham, Isaac,

Jacob, Joseph, Joshua, Rahab, Gideon, Barak, Samson, David, and the prophets cheering us on in the stands.

And then there is our amazing Jesus. We need to remember all He endured and all He gained by obedience and faithfulness to God and devoted love to us.

God Gives Us Free Will

It is a profound sadness that many who have been given and promised much choose to give up of their own accord. In Daniel 5 we read that King Belshazzar inherited the kingdom of Babylon from King Nebuchadnezzar. This was a huge privilege and an awesome responsibility. But pride entered the king's heart. He forgot what was sacred and indulged his flesh, becoming arrogant in his God-appointed position.

In verse 14 we see that Belshazzar hosted an enormous banquet for one thousand of his nobles. During the feasting and drinking, he called for the gold and silver goblets that his father had taken from the temple in Jerusalem. These were sacred cups set aside for God. As they drank wine from these holy cups, they praised the gods of silver, gold, bronze, iron, wood, and stone. As he publicly blasphemed the living God in this outrageous way, a finger appeared and wrote on the plaster of the wall. It was an eerie and terrifying scene. The king sent for all his wise men to try to interpret the writing, but only Daniel could read the message.

In Daniel 5:23–24, Daniel reveals to the king what the hand wrote on the wall: "You did not honor the God who holds in his hand your life and all your ways. Therefore he sent the hand that

wrote the inscription." The message was one of divine wrath, and
that very night Belshazzar was killed and his kingdom given to
another.

In our own lives, we may not blatantly blaspheme the Lord and
worship other gods; it may just be that we are quietly happy with our
lives and accomplishments and not interested in devoting ourselves
to Him. We like things just the way they are … and God might make
things uncomfortable. But remember that plan full of opportunity
and promise designed and shaped just for you! God asks us to choose
to honor Him in every part of our lives, in every decision we make,
and in the way we let Him define every day of our lives. God longs
for us to *choose* to seek Him, to actively run after Him and take hold
of all He has for us. With everything we have, let's not miss all that
God holds in His hands for us!

Seeking God's Face

*"Then you will call upon me and come and pray to me, and I will
listen to you." (Jer. 29:12)*

Ask Him to speak to you, to tell you His plans for your life—*and
He will!* God wants you to come and pray to Him, He wants you to
talk to Him about the things that matter to you. As you do that, you
are able to choose Him over comfort, over stability, over the material
things that the world has to offer.

We ended up moving to America a while ago. All the things we
had prayed and labored for in the UK were starting to happen. We

had sweet community in an idyllic part of the country. Our families were around the corner, our children were happy at school, and our life was set for the next fifteen to twenty years. But we started to sense God prompting a time of transition for us … but what, where, and how would we ever leave this beautiful place?

We decided that we would get up early and pray together.

Now don't get me wrong—I think settling in one place requires amazing character and huge commitment. In many ways it's easier to be a pioneer than a settler. However, in this instance, while we had everything to stay for, still we knew "we live once, we're only young once, and if God is leading us, then we need to go."

Setting the alarm clock before 6 a.m. made me feel really holy.

On the first day when the alarm went off I thought, *maybe tomorrow*. Out of the corner of my eye I saw Matt's feet rolling out of the duvet and onto the floor. That was my encouragement to get out of bed and start praying to the God who, as it says in Daniel, "holds in his hands [our] life and all [our] ways." My flesh was weak (I am *so* not a morning person), but my spirit said *yes!* I opened the Bible, prayed, and wrote down some verses. It wasn't rocket science, and there was no finger writing on the wall, but slowly and surely as the weeks went on, I felt my faith growing, and all the verses I wrote down began to formulate a theme. In fact, we both separately got that same sense about a possible change. We tried to fill in the gaps in the flesh, to decide what God "must be saying"—but then I read a powerful verse, Proverbs 16:9, that put me in my place:

> *In his heart a man plans his course,*
> *but the LORD determines his steps.*

Very often the flesh can't wait to join the dots way before the spirit is ready to unveil things.

Later, a good friend of ours from Atlanta came to visit. He was just popping in for the afternoon, and we were excited to catch up. After some small talk he told us about what God was doing in Atlanta, Georgia. I had absolutely no idea before the conversation began that our chat would lead us to pack up our whole house, sell our home, and leave the UK nine months later to live in America! Yet by the end of the conversation, both Matt and I wondered separately if this was the place God had been nudging us toward.

I had so many questions, but I knew now was not the time. The next thing we did was *wait* for God's plans to unfold. The waiting was excruciating, particularly for someone of my character! When I make a decision, I'm ready to go straight ahead with it and have it happen immediately! I really am a "make it happen" kind of person, but clearly in this instance I needed to stop myself and exercise wisdom and patience.

The Bible is full of exhortations to wait upon God. Psalm 38:15 says, "I wait for you, O LORD; you will answer, O LORD my God." Matt has an amazing gift of waiting and pondering things, but I have a very big mouth! When an angel appeared to Mary and revealed the news that she was to become the mother of the Son of God, the Bible says she "pondered [those things] in her heart" (Luke 2:19). I think it's crucial for us women (me especially) to pause for a minute and take hold of that. We can discredit and even humiliate ourselves if we say everything we think.

I know a woman who every few weeks announces to the world her latest plans. Over the years it became evident that these were just

spoken thoughts rather than dreams and plans that had been pondered and weighed, because not one of them ever came to pass. As I
first thought we might start something new, I could have destroyed
God's plans by dissecting my thoughts and excitedly looking to others for their approval. I have learned much from Mary, and from my
amazing husband, particularly that I must wait to act and especially
to speak. Pondering is an absolute must if we are to dream big dreams
and be trusted with much.

As many weeks passed, we prayed, and I bit my lip and asked
very specifically for a sign to confirm that we were indeed to move
to America. We prayed for "something that we could hold in our
hands."

One night as we were stuck in traffic we prayed boldly, again
asking God for a sign directing us clearly to Atlanta. When we got
home, a parcel was waiting on the doorstep. Matt opened it and
started laughing. Inside was an oversized mug that in large capital letters spelled out "Atlanta." Amazingly, someone who had stayed with
us months before wanted to send a thank-you present and, while in
America, saw the mug in a coffee shop and was prompted to put it
in the post. Our mug is now on the piano in our home in Atlanta!
When I look at it I can't help but laugh. God confirmed His plans
for our life in a specific, tangible, and funny way. He answered our
prayer for something that we could hold in our hands—a *Starbucks
mug!* God is in control of events, and when you seek Him with all
your heart, the Bible says, you find Him!

He is faithful!

When you are faced with situations that feel like mountains
you can't climb, or a decision you simply don't know how to make,

remember that our God is a God who moves mountains and causes the miraculous to happen. When He opens a door, no one can shut it. If God tells a wound to heal, He will be faithful, and healing happens! There have been so many times we have clung to both our sanity and our faith by our fingernails, but faith and trust in God Almighty brought us through. When He caused us to consider a "transfer," He knew He would be sending us to Atlanta—but He waited until we were willing and ready, and then He caused the right things to fall into place at the right time. He works in miraculous ways in our lives. God in His grace supplies all our needs according to His glorious riches in Christ Jesus.

So going back to where we started—your lane in the race and the challenge before you. You are beautiful, and you and your lane have something in common: *You overflow with destiny and promise!* Dress light for the race, trust your choices to God … and you will run freely. Don't worry about who's running next to you and their privileges and opportunities. My little boy's favorite phrase at the moment is "it's not fair." He continually comes to me when he thinks his siblings have an unfair advantage, and he looks to me for justice! You and I need to faithfully trust God in times when our race feels unfair and continue looking to our almighty God. Let's keep a humble attitude and remain focused on the prize and the eternal promise of heaven.

When you feel the burn, *keep going*. God sees your choices, and He will reward you, help you, and trust you with much as you press on toward the goal!

So seek Him, keep your eyes on Him, and run, baby, run!

Chapter Five

GOD HAS NOT FORGOTTEN ME

The idea that God could ever forget us is simply a feeling, not a reality. If you've ever felt like that, you are not alone, but God's truth can permeate the strongest feelings. We know from the Word of God that though we may not always understand every circumstance we find ourselves in, He will never forsake us. It is important that we look at what causes us to feel that God has forgotten us and remedy those destructive thoughts by soaking our minds in truth.

Thoughts of abandonment and rage can easily surface in the absence of answered prayer and relief, but we must not let the Enemy use them to destroy truth. God will never leave you or forsake you! *End of story.*

When God Is Silent: God Speaks His Word to Me

Answer me when I call to you, O my righteous God. Give me relief from my distress; be merciful to me and hear my prayer. (Ps. 4:1)

It's true—we've all been there. When we feel that God is not answering our prayers, seeing someone else's answer to prayer can feel like rubbing salt in an open wound rather than an encouragement to keep pressing into Jesus.

When the desires of our hearts remain unfulfilled, we can experience a false sense of not being heard or favored by God. As daughters, we need to know that our Father hears us.

Psalm 28:1 speaks of a desperation to hear God speak: "To you I call, O LORD my Rock; do not turn a deaf ear to me. For if you remain silent, I will be like those who have gone down to the pit." Indeed, there are times when the psalmist truly relates to this "forgotten" sentiment. He agonizes at God's apparent silence. In Psalm 22:2 he writes, "O my God, I cry out by day, but you do not answer."

Sometimes God is silent; He does not come through for us immediately, and we are called to persevere in faith and wait patiently for Him. In those times when our circumstances rage, it may indeed appear as though we are forgotten. Some spend years forging ahead, being faithful, and waiting for a call that doesn't come. When our prayers appear unheard and we presume the absence of God, *we have to push through to the facts.*

In times of silence, God's Word can always speak to us. Therefore, though you may be crushed, perplexed, on guard, and perhaps angry, it is vital to keep reading Scripture on a daily basis. You must feed your soul with life and not let the Enemy use your feelings to deceive you. A heart open to hearing God's voice is a heart close to breakthrough. The Word is truth, and the truth brings freedom.

If you are looking for breakthrough on a specific issue, *ask* for it. Sometimes we need to ask God to speak to us in a specific way. As we ask, there are many times we have to be patient and wait for an answer, but God is faithful; He will answer you at the right time.

When the Door Is Shut: God Says Wait

But those who wait for the Lord [who expect, look for, and hope in Him] shall change and renew their strength and power; they shall lift their wings and mount up [close to God] as eagles [mount up to the sun]; they shall run and not be weary, they shall walk and not faint or become tired. (Isa. 40:31 AB)

So we know from Scripture that we are to wait for God. Psalm 40:1 demonstrates not just the act of waiting but also possessing the right spiritual attitude too. It says, "I waited *patiently* for the LORD; he turned to me and heard my cry." This underlines the importance of patience!

If you are lacking patience as you wait, ask God and seek Him for the gift of patience. When Jesus left His disciples, His primary instruction was to "wait for the gift my Father promised, which you have heard me speak about" (Acts 1:4).

Waiting on God also shows a level of faith that honors Him. Then God graciously credits that faith to us as righteousness. Patience is basically an attitude that trusts beyond circumstances and desires, that if God has promised something, He will carry out that promise. Patience ushers in our peace. In fact, Abraham, the first man with whom God made a covenant, waited until he was one hundred years old to receive the son and heir God had promised him many years before.

In our waiting, our faith is stretched and tested. We see *how* the disciples went about waiting: "All of these with their minds in full agreement devoted themselves steadfastly to prayer [waiting together] with the women and Mary the mother of Jesus, and with His brothers" (Acts 1:14 AB). The disciples did not question where the Holy Spirit was or doubt all that Jesus told them. No, although the Holy Spirit did not come immediately, they devoted themselves to prayer and to waiting patiently with undeviating constancy and resolve. They didn't just wait for a day—they waited for weeks! Just because you don't see the answer to your prayers right now, this month, or this year, does not mean the answer is not coming. It just means you're still waiting. The key to receiving the promises of God is in the waiting, trusting, hoping, and believing.

When I Am in Need: God Is My Provider

God said to Moses, "I am who I am. This is what you are to say to the Israelites: 'I AM has sent me to you.'" (Ex. 3:14)

So we see this annoying thing called "waiting" will actually develop our character as through it we learn to trust in God and have patience for His timing. God is the great *I Am*. Another way of understanding "I Am" is to think of God saying I Am whatever you need. I Am your father if you are fatherless, I Am your patience when you are impatient. I Am your healer when you are sick, I Am your provider when you are without. As we articulate to the great I Am what we need I Am to be in our life, He will hear us and provide us with what we need.

Jesus taught us to ask God each day for our daily needs: "Give us today our daily bread" (Matt. 6:11). At that time, bread was the basic staple food that everyone lived on. Even today we understand that bread is one of the staples of our diet. Then in John 6:35 Jesus declares: "I *am* the bread of life. He who comes to me will never go hungry, and he who believes in me will never be thirsty." Jesus teaches us to ask for everything that we need, because He is all that we need. He is the basic requirement for you in your life today. God is the provider of all that we need—*all we have to do is ask.*

When I Am in Trouble: God Hears Me

Is any one of you in trouble? He should pray. (James 5:13)

When we are suffering, in trouble, doubting, or banging away on a door that seems to be firmly closed, sometimes instead of going straight to God, instead of talking to heaven, we can start grumbling. When we complain about how terrible our circumstances are and say how awful things are, we can begin to question whether God is who He says He is. Suddenly we find ourselves questioning His promises, His goodness, and His plan for our lives.

We have to remember our own feelings can deceive us. Sometimes we convince ourselves that something is from God, when really it's just ourselves. Many times prayers that I felt should have been answered were just my own thoughts that I tried to tag God onto! We have to be humble and trust. We shouldn't set up for ourselves a fantasy world of things we are convinced God promised us. We don't need to condemn ourselves or overanalyze—let's just be rooted in the truth and ask God to show and confirm His will.

In the midst of silence or doubt, we have a choice. We either choose to converse with others, question God's goodness, and agree with the lies of the Enemy, or we can take the conversation straight to God. When we start wondering where in the world God is, *voice it to Him!* Articulate it and ask God to His face: *Where are You? Is this me? Are You telling me to wait patiently, or am I off?* He can handle your questions!

Remember when Jesus called out to God the Father as He hung in agony on the cross: "My God, my God, why have you forsaken me?" (Matt. 27:46). Jesus has been there—He felt as though God left Him, abandoned Him, and deserted Him. While hanging on the cross, not only was He in physical agony, but He was also in spiritual distress—because for the first time He did not feel the presence of His Father. This demonstrates that it is possible to be in the middle of God's will, doing what He has called you to do, find it the hardest thing you have ever done, and still *not* feel His presence with you. Ask Him for confirmation and affirmation.

In the middle of all Jesus went through He cried out to God from His heart, using Psalm 22 as His reference point. Although Jesus only spoke the first line, Psalm 22 profoundly fits the circumstances of Jesus at the crucifixion, describing in detail His agony—"I am poured out like water, and all my bones are out of joint" (v. 14)—and yet it ends with such hope: "For he has not despised or disdained the suffering of the afflicted one; he has not hidden his face from him, but has listened to his cry for help" (v. 24). God did not save Jesus from death that day. Rather He resurrected Him on the third day, and in so doing, defeated death and the Enemy and brought about a new covenant for all people for the forgiveness of sins.

But God heard and affirmed His faithful Son. Similarly, God hears us in our darkest places. The gospel of Matthew sheds amazing revelation and insight regarding our prayer lives:

> *"But when you pray, go into your [most] private room, and, closing the door, pray to your Father, Who is in secret; and your Father, Who sees in secret, will reward you in the open. And when you pray, do not heap up phrases (multiply words, repeating the same ones over and over) as the Gentiles do, for they think they will be heard for their much speaking. Do not be like them, for your Father knows what you need before you ask Him." (Matt. 6:6–8 AB)*

Jesus says we should talk to our heavenly Father like we would talk to a normal person. We shouldn't speak to Him like an ancient character from one of Chaucer's novels! We can cry out to Him: *Help, Father, I am in crisis, the Enemy is tempting me, my heart is low and full of doubt.* Be real, be raw, and speak to God as your most trusted friend. He hears the cries of your heart, because He knows you; He knows what you are asking for. We can tell Him everything, even the stuff that might shock others. He will never reject us. However, being real doesn't mean being rude, and we must remember that we are speaking to the God of heaven and earth—reverence is to coexist with our raw heart cries! Isaiah 65:24 says, "Before they call I will answer; while they are still speaking I will hear."

He hears you—whether you hear Him or not! Will He hear you moaning or humbling yourself and seeking His face? When we desire to hear from God, being on our knees and seeking His face is a good place to start.

When I Doubt: God Is Faithful

For the LORD is good and his love endures forever; his faithfulness continues through all generations. (Ps. 100:5)

Sadly, there is an Enemy who can to speak to us and who longs to dent and discourage our faith—to use our confusion to bring wounds against God. Indeed, Satan takes every opportunity to drip deadly poison into your soul through his words. Each time you harbor a doubt or a question in your mind and decide to deal with it on your own or let it fester instead of taking it to God, the Enemy has an opportunity. He wants to form a wedge between you and God. He can cause a bruise and make that doubt, that nagging fear or worry about the future bigger and bigger in your mind. Soon you will believe his words and agree with the unbelief that so easily takes hold, unless you are alert and active to the schemes of the Devil. Again, we have a choice of whom we believe—God, the

Enemy, or ourselves. The Enemy tells you that you are forgotten, that God doesn't really exist or care about you, because if He did He would have come through for you by now or answered your prayers. *God is not to be trusted!* the Enemy shouts. Temptation looms.

How do we know that these are lies from the pit of hell? Because that is not what the Bible says! That is not who our God is. God is kind and trustworthy! The Enemy speaks his lies of death over us in order to confuse us and contradict all that we know is true of the Lord from His Word. The most powerful antidote to doubt is faith. Proverbs 13:12 says, "Hope deferred makes the heart sick, but a longing fulfilled is a tree of life." In times of suffering, silence from God or trials can really test and stretch our faith as we question God's voice and His character.

Hebrews 11:1 says, "Now faith is being sure of what we hope for and certain of what we do not see." Faith is a decision to believe the things and the Word of God rather than our own unbelief or the Enemy's lies.

Indeed, the amount of faith we have can directly influence the work that God can do in our lives. Many times throughout the gospels, Jesus remarks at the levels of faith that people have. In Matthew 15:28 Jesus remarks on the faith of the Canaanite woman: "'Woman, you have great faith! Your request is granted.' And her daughter was healed from that very hour." And there were even villages where Jesus did not do many signs or wonders because of the people's lack of faith. The *New Dictionary of Theology* defines scriptural faith as "both an attitude of spirit which we freely exercise, and the gift of God."[1] We can therefore *practice* trusting in God for all that we need and, in so doing, develop and build up our faith. We can also, like the disciples, ask God for more faith: "The apostles said to the Lord, 'Increase our faith!'" (Luke 17:5). Our faith glorifies God and is an attitude that blesses Him, moving Him to respond. As Hebrews 11:6 says, "Without faith, it is impossible to please God, because anyone who comes to him must believe that he exists and that he rewards those who earnestly seek him."

It is worth checking our hearts and minds and asking ourselves, *Whose voice am I listening to?* Are we persevering in our faith and doing the things we know feed our souls and our faith? Being faithful is like keeping fit—you've got to put in the training if you want to be fit for the race. Staying in shape means going to the gym or working out regularly, and if you stop doing that, you'll get out of shape!

After five pregnancies I can confirm that if you are not careful you will get flabby. After each baby is safely delivered, the only way for me to stay fit is a workout—a regular, disciplined exercise program. That is the only reason I can actually do up the buttons on any of my skinny jeans! My body did not ping back; I had to work not only to get fit but also to stay in my clothes … *to remain fit.* It's like that with our faith, sista! If your faith is a little flabby right now, get into truth and get back in spiritual shape. Faith needs to be practiced regularly in order to keep our relationship with God fresh for today.

Doubt does not have to disable us from crying out to God to save us as Peter did when he was walking on the water: "When he saw the wind, he was afraid and, beginning to sink, cried out, 'Lord, save me!'" (Matt. 14:30). In His mercy and grace, Jesus immediately "reached out his hand and caught him. 'You of little faith,' he said, 'why did you doubt?'" (v. 31).

Your doubt won't stop Him from coming to rescue you!

Speak the Truth into Your Circumstances

"I, the LORD, speak the truth; I declare what is right." (Isa. 45:19)

Psalm 102 is "a prayer of one overwhelmed with trouble, pouring out problems before the LORD" (NLT)—and does David have some problems! This passage tells us that he is in complete despair emotionally, spiritually, and physically. His enemies are mocking him, and at night his tears spill down into his drink. He is hungry, aching, in agony, lonely, defenseless, and homeless, and until verse 11 we hear how troubled he is when he says, "My heart is sick, withered like grass, and I have lost my appetite" (v. 4). His circumstances are so overwhelmingly bad that they affect him mentally and physically.

This is a painfully accurate description of times of pain, loneliness, and suffering. If you are unable to eat because a situation is eating you up with worry, if your pillow is wet from tears late at night, if you wake early in the morning sick with anxiety about the circumstances you face, or if your heart races with grief, you can relate to these feelings David movingly describes in Scripture.

The way David deals with these circumstances is to acknowledge them before God, state the facts, verbalize how he feels, and cry out from the depths of his soul to God. Then he makes a very important internal decision. He switches his attention away from his circumstances and his problems ... to the eternal, the Almighty: "But you, O LORD, sit enthroned forever; your renown endures through all generations" (Ps. 102:12). Here David begins to look up from the pit into the heavenly realm. He starts to remember who God is. The fact of the matter is that what he is going through is horrible but temporary. He remembers God's mercy, how He has moved in his life before, and how God is able to do that again. Something eternal and wonderful will happen.

Then we see a dramatic shift in the first verse of Psalm 103, when David says, "Let all that I am praise the LORD" (Ps. 103:1 NLT). David speaks to himself, saying, "Wait—this is what my circumstance and my feelings tell me, but my spirit is coming to a higher place!" He had the potential to deceive himself and to say, "Where I am at means that God is unfaithful." But he pushed through to a place of empowerment and embraced the living Word of truth. He broke through!

He goes on to say, "with my whole heart, I will praise his holy name ... [and] never forget the good things he does for me" (Ps. 103:1–2 NLT). Then David begins to list all the good things God does for him. His bones were burning like red-hot coals, so he calls the Lord his Healer—in the midst of being sick he says, "Excuse me, I will tell myself, *God is a healer.*" Is he a mad man? No, he is defeating the Enemy's scheme. David tells himself what God is going to do for him—speaking God's goodness into every situation that needs Him. So in Psalm 102 he is speaking from a place of abandonment and near death. In Psalm 103 we hear how God "redeems your life from the pit ... [and] satisfies your desires with good things so that your youth is renewed like the eagle's" (Ps. 103:4–5). He speaks to each specific problem and submits it to the authority and truth of who God is.

If you feel that your lane is leading you along a dark and lonely tunnel right now, look back over Psalm 23. Name all the things you need *I Am* to be for you—your shepherd, your leader, your provider, your restorer, your guide, your comfort, your helper, and your anointer. Take a look at that dark valley of Psalm 23—*where is God?*

He is *in* the valley, *in* the presence of your enemies, *in* front of those people who rejected you and who said you couldn't do it, and *in* front of your own fears and failures. Psalm 23 shows us that despite the valley, despite the circumstances and the pain, God has not abandoned you or forgotten you. *No!*

He has prepared an amazing banquet for you. There is a beautiful feast there for you to enjoy in the presence of your enemies. Jesus is right there with you. *Eat and be filled!*

Speak the Truth to the Enemy

Finally, be strong in the Lord and in his mighty power. Put on the full armor of God so that you can take your stand against the devil's schemes. (Eph. 6:10–11)

As we speak the truth of Scripture to ourselves, we are also speaking the truth of God to the Enemy and, in so doing, *silencing him.* This is not just lackluster positive thinking; this is a powerful, biblical tool of spiritual warfare that Jesus Christ used when He was tempted in the desert. After forty days of fasting, Jesus was hungry, and the

Devil used this opportunity to tempt Him when He was at His very weakest in the flesh. Each time the Devil tempted Him, Jesus replied with Scripture, saying such things as, "It is written: 'Man does not live on bread alone'" (Luke 4:4).

If Jesus Christ needed to use Scripture to resist the Enemy, we need to use it too! We see both in Genesis, when the Enemy successfully tempts Eve, and in the desert, when he unsuccessfully tempts Christ, that the Enemy has a voice. He will speak to you and lie. He will twist the words of God—as in Genesis 3:1 when he asks Eve, "Did God really say, 'You must not eat from any tree in the garden'?" and in Luke 4:10 when he quotes Psalm 91:11–12 in order to try to tempt Jesus. By causing Eve to doubt God, the Enemy succeeded in tempting her, and the course of human history changed forever. But by holding firm to the truth of God, and specifically by using Scripture correctly, Jesus resisted the Enemy and continued to resist temptation until His resurrection, reversing the curse brought on humanity through Adam and Eve.

Let us understand, then, that we do face testing times, and there will be inevitable temptation from the Enemy. We can resist this temptation by using the Bible as a form of "kick butt" defense. James 4:7 says, "Resist the devil, and he will flee from you." Jesus resisted verbally and *out loud*, and this is key: It is important to verbalize Scripture. Don't just keep it in your head, *but shout it out* at the Devil, at your circumstances, over yourself, and in praise to God! Scripture is an amazing weapon that will cause the heaviness over your life to spontaneously combust!

The ring on my mobile phone is annoyingly persistent; it just goes on and on and on—bleeping, ringing loudly until I stop whatever I am doing and get up and physically turn it off. That is what the Enemy is like. He is a persistent, nagging, tempting liar, and he will not stop until you resist him with Scripture and tell him to flee. You must tell him! God gave you both the words and the authority to speak! When we pray and proclaim Scripture we not only declare it to ourselves, we declare it to the heavenly realm. Ephesians 6:17 says, "Take the helmet of salvation and the sword of the Spirit, which is the word of God." These are our tools to fight with. The Word of God enables us to fight and win battles in our lives that the Enemy wants us to lose. However, a sword is not much use if you never get it out! We need to have a thorough working knowledge of Scripture in order to wield it correctly in battle in all areas of our life.

We are also to pray, "Lead us not into temptation, but deliver us from the evil one" (Matt. 6:13). Again, Jesus is all we need. He is the one who delivers us from evil and from the temptation of the Devil. He has been tempted and has resisted the Enemy. We must do the same. Resist the Enemy through the power of Christ in you. Tell him that he is a liar and speak the truth of God over your life and your circumstances. Look at the cross of Christ, look at His hands of love where your name is goodness, mercy, and love that He has lavished upon you.

Check Your Heart for Unconfessed Sin

If we claim to be without sin, we deceive ourselves and the truth is not in us. If we confess our sins, he is faithful and just and will forgive us our sins and purify us from all unrighteousness. *(1 John 1:8–9)*

When we are looking for a breakthrough in our lives, it is important to check that there are no unconfessed sins, or sins against us left unforgiven, that are preventing us from hearing God. When Jesus teaches us how to pray, He focuses particularly on forgiving others. The Amplified Bible puts it like this:

> *"If you forgive people their trespasses [their reckless and willful sins, leaving them, letting them go, and giving up resentment], your heavenly Father will also forgive you. But if you do not forgive others their trespasses [their reckless and willful sins, leaving them, letting them go, and giving up resentment], neither will your Father forgive you your trespasses." (Matt. 6:14–15 AB)*

When we are lost, God comes to find us and removes the sense of separation between Him and us. He forgives us our sins in order that we can have an intimate friendship with Him. He therefore asks us to forgive others their sins, so that we can be in relationship with our brothers and sisters. Holding on to unforgiven sins in our hearts prevents us being in relationship with others and with God. That grieves God immensely.

In Matthew 18 Jesus tells the parable of the unmerciful servant to show us what this kind of unforgiven sin looks like. A servant owed a king a huge sum of money. The king took pity on him, canceled the debt, and let him go. However, this same servant, when he came across another servant who owed him a small amount of money, refused to show mercy and had him thrown into jail. This deeply distressed the other servants, who reported his behavior to the king. The king called the servant in before him and said, "You wicked servant ... I canceled all that debt of yours because you begged me to. Shouldn't you have had mercy on your fellow servant just as I had on you?" (Matt. 18:32–33). In anger the king "turned him over to the jailers to be tortured, until he should pay back all he owed" (v. 34). Jesus ends the parable by saying, "This is how my heavenly Father will treat each of you unless you forgive your brother from your heart" (v. 35).

Not forgiving others is very much like a torture of the heart. It means you *hold on* to resentment, the wrongs done to you, and the words spoken over you. Withholding forgiveness from others means God withholds His forgiveness from you—and a barrier is built up in our relationship with God. A barrier entirely of our own making, which can prevent the way God hears our prayers and affects our future. Forgiving that person means releasing yourself from the memory of what has been done to you. Let go, move on, and forgive as you yourself have been forgiven. Then God will be able to release His forgiveness to you, speak to you, lead you, and direct you in all goodness and truth. Give yourself the best chance of receiving all the good things God has for you by releasing those who have hurt you and getting right with God. His plans for us are exceptional and stunning, so I am constantly reminding myself not to self-sabotage by withholding any forgiveness from others. Let's not allow ourselves to be robbed or unwittingly rob ourselves. Let's get right and get ready for what's next as we pray with hope and wait patiently—let's fight the good fight and win. Amen!

Some Scriptures for the Fight

All scripture is God-breathed and is useful for teaching, rebuking, correcting and training in righteousness. (2 Tim. 3:16)

And God is able to make all grace abound to you, so that in all things at all times, having all that you need, you will abound in every good work. (2 Cor. 9:8)

Jesus looked at them and said, "With man this is impossible, but with God all things are possible." (Matt. 19:26)

There is now no condemnation for those who are in Christ Jesus, because through Christ Jesus the law of the Sprit of life set me free from the law of sin and death. (Rom. 8:1–2)

If God is for us, who can be against us? He who did not spare his own Son, but gave him up for us all—how will he not also, along

*with him, graciously give us all things? (Rom.
8:31–32)*

*No, in all these things we are more than
conquerors through him who loved us. For
I am convinced that neither death nor life,
neither angels nor demons, neither the present
nor the future, nor any powers, neither height
nor depth, nor anything else in all creation,
will be able to separate us from the love of
God that is in Christ Jesus our Lord. (Rom.
8:37–39)*

*Praise be to the God and Father of our Lord Jesus
Christ, the Father of compassion and the God of
all comfort, who comforts us in all our troubles,
so that we can comfort those in any trouble with
the comfort we ourselves have received from God.
(2 Cor. 1:3–4)*

*Be strong and take heart, all you who hope in the
LORD. (Ps. 31:24)*

*I waited patiently for the LORD; he turned to me
and heard my cry. (Ps. 40:1)*

*The Lord knows how to rescue godly men from
trials. (2 Peter 2:9)*

The second son he named Ephraim and said, "It is because God has made me fruitful in the land of my suffering." (Gen. 41:52)

My comfort in my suffering is this: Your promise preserves my life. (Ps. 119:50)

I am still confident of this: I will see the goodness of the LORD in the land of the living. Wait for the LORD, be strong and take heart and wait for the LORD. (Ps. 27:14)

Chapter Six

GOD IS MY HELPER

Come On, Girl—You Can Do It!

The LORD is my strength and my song; he has become my salvation.
(Ps. 118:14)

Life is tough. It is relentless. Human beings are pretty high maintenance, and survival can be exhausting at times. But we are called to do more than survive—we are called to *thrive!* So let's run our race with perseverance, take up our cross, and follow Jesus, telling others about Him and living in a way that honors Him, serves Him, and gives glory to Him.

Sometimes, it can all seem to be a bit tiring, but He has shown us that He can be our strength—Christ *in* you is the hope of glory! *We have hope!* Christ is indeed *in* us, with us, available to us, and as Philippians 4:13 says, "I can do everything through him who gives me strength." When we feel overwhelmed with all there is to do, prepare, pray about, forgive, lay down, take up, put on, deal with, wash, clean, and pay for, we can call on the Lord for strength to face the day!

Isaiah 40:31 tells us, "Those who hope in the LORD will renew their strength." To "hope in" means to wait expectantly. *Renew* means literally "to exchange"—so the Bible tells us that *as we hope in God*, we exchange, renew, or change out our weakness, exhaustion, and inability *into God's strength*. Isaiah then gets specific about how God strengthens us: "They will soar on wings like eagles; they will run and not grow weary, they will walk and not be faint." Here we have an amazing promise from God of complete supernatural strength and power to do His will. Eagles were known for their vigor, energy, and speed.

The Bible also uses the eagle as a picture of God carrying and protecting His people in Exodus 19:4: "You yourselves have seen what I did to Egypt, and how I carried you on eagles' wings and brought you to myself." A golden eagle's average wingspan is six to seven and a half feet, and their wings are long and broad, enabling them to soar effectively. What a mighty picture of supernatural rescue! God says He comes from outside of our situation to carry us on wings like eagles, to a place of safety.

Isaiah 30:15 promises, "This is what the Sovereign LORD, the Holy One of Israel, says: 'In repentance and rest is your salvation, in quietness and trust is your strength.'" As we meditate on these scriptures, we can exchange our exhaustion for His strength, our downheartedness for His hope, and our feelings of being overwhelmed for the knowledge that we can do *all* things through Christ who strengthens us.

When you can't do it, He can and *He will!*

Warriors and Angels

God is our refuge and strength, an ever-present help in trouble. (Ps. 46:1)

When the Bible tells us that God is an ever-present help in times of trouble, it is literal in all circumstances in our lives today. We can know God as our helper for both comfort and growth. God gave us Himself in the form of the Holy Spirit.

When we read the psalms of David we remember that even when our circumstances fail us, God is always available and ready to help the children that He loves. He is an *ever-present help.* He is strength in our weakness, wisdom in our confusion, and grace in our folly. In seasons of uncertainty or frailty, God is near and ready when we call!

As I go about my day, sometimes I call out loudly to my husband for help. The problem is he's a busy man with a big life, and clearly he can't always drop everything and come running. Admittedly, at times my tone can become both annoying and whiny as my call for him becomes more fervent! He knows that when I shout for him, I have hit a wall that is too much for me, and so, if he is available, eventually he gets up to see what I need.

I'm *so* grateful for that help, but Matt, like all human beings, is not available twenty-four hours a day or every time I need him. So I have become used to long seasons of separation and learned to flex my independence muscles in the home and in my life. However, there are occasions when I am ill or overloaded and I need help. *Who can I call on then? Who can I rely on in those moments?*

The secret of my strength is the Lord.

Clearly and quite beautifully, the Bible reassures us that Jesus, by the presence of the Holy Spirit, is *always* near and His ears are open when we cry, *Help!* Amazingly, He responds as our personal deliverer. I'm so grateful for the times I have no one to rely on and my *self* is not enough, because it is in those moments when I call out, *Help!* that I rediscover the Giver of life.

As we turn to Him we put Him first as Lord and acknowledge our own inadequacies. We remember that we were made for relationship and reliance on our Father God. As we call out in dependence, the Spirit of truth speaks back to us, and in faith and trust we find ourselves receiving direct provision, specific correction, and perfect wisdom from above. *He is near!* Even when no one is there in the physical, we can encounter a miraculous dimension of His strong arms and the comfort of His astounding peace. It is because of Him that I can go beyond my natural abilities and deal with life in all its occasional grimness with my head lifted high and without despair— not because I have learned to be superwoman, but because I have found Jesus, my ever-present help, the One who hears me when I call and the One who meets me in my hour of need, in seasons where I have no direction.

Psalm 91:1–2 says, "He who dwells in the shelter of the Most High will rest in the shadow of the Almighty. I will say of the LORD, 'He is my refuge and my fortress, my God, in whom I trust.'"

Our spiritual battle is fought daily in our circumstances, our feelings, our emotions, and our troubles. Here the psalmist boldly declares that God is his refuge and his shelter. He affirms and declares to himself that it is God who will protect him, not a castle or a strong army. The Lord Almighty offers him safety, security, and protection. As we trust in God we will rise up and become soldier girls! We are independent, yet totally dependent, and strong in the Spirit! As His soldier I'm leading others, but I'm not the leader; I'm tough, but I'm not hardened; and I'm full of power but not in control. As we lean on His help we'll find that we can stand up against any emotion and fight any lie with truth!

God equips us to fight in this battle by giving us the sword of the Spirit, which is the Word of God (Eph. 6:17). We can always declare that trust in Him over our lives, and as we do, we learn that He is the only one we can depend on. He helps us again by giving us the truth to stand on. Feelings can deceive us. We can be enticed into shutting down, holding back, or even giving up; but if we take our feelings to Him for clarity, support, and freedom, He is the most secure place for us to hide.

Women sometimes joke about themselves or others by calling someone a "drama queen." I can't bear that term because it sounds so shameful. I heard it put more kindly when someone said, "People with strong feelings continually create their own tornadoes!" Instead of living like all-feeling, wailing tornadoes, we become the *calm in the storm* by allowing Him into our trouble—because He becomes the calm for us. The good news is that if we hide ourselves in Him, His calm peace comes upon us despite whatever is still raging around us.

Another weapon in our armor is trust in God. If we insist on trusting our jobs, our houses, or our own abilities to provide a way out of trouble, we will always remain anxious women who are only really working for ourselves. As the global economic crisis recently demonstrated, everything you have worked for, lived for, and depended on can be stripped away in a matter of hours. That includes your job, your business, your bank balance, and the very bank itself! If you don't put God first and have your trust in Him as the center when things fall or people fail you, *what do you have to stand on and trust in?*

In Matthew 7 Jesus talks about the wise and the foolish builders. The wise builder built his house on the rock. When the storm came, the house stood firm because its foundations were firmly rooted to the rock. But the foolish builder built his house on the sand. When the rains came, the house collapsed because the foundations were useless. The foolish man *heard* the teachings of Jesus—but failed to *put them into practice*. He did not build his life on Jesus, trusting in Him for everything. When his faith was tested, the foundations were worthless, and so the house fell down with an almighty crash.

The storm, the wind, and the rain are all symbolic of the troubles, pressures, and problems that we will face in our lives. Jesus does not say that if you build your house on the rock you will *escape* the storm. Rather, if you build your house on the rock you will be able to *withstand* the storm. As we build our lives, our plans, and our dreams on Jesus, trusting in Him for all that we hope and long for, we will be able to stand strong in our faith regardless of whatever "weather" comes our way. We can call on Him for His help in times of trouble and for wisdom as we move forward in our journey of faith through life.

Only the Lord Almighty is a strong fortress worthy of all our trust. He is the rock who will never be shaken, the owner of sheep on a thousand hills, the Lord Almighty in battle. Psalm 91 shows us that we can trust God to rescue us from disease, attack, and enemies—*anything*, in fact! This trust in God is counted as faith, which Ephesians calls "the shield of faith, with which you can extinguish all the flaming arrows of the evil one" (6:16). But this attitude of trust and faith is not just a defensive weapon: It actually delights the heart of God. Right at the end of Psalm 91 the narrative switches from the psalmist to God, and in verses 14 and 15 God responds: "'Because he loves me,' says the LORD, 'I will rescue him; I will protect him, for he acknowledges my name. He will call upon me, and I will answer him; I will be with him in trouble, I will deliver him and honor him.'"

God sees us in our trouble, God rescues us from trouble, and then He honors us for our faith and trust in Him during our trouble.

Let us remember that God is the Head of a mighty army. Isaiah 42:13 says, "The LORD will march out like a mighty man, like a warrior he will stir up his zeal; with a shout he will raise the battle cry and will triumph over his enemies." Like Aslan roaring back to life and rallying the troops of Narnia behind him as he vanquishes the White Witch, we too can rise up and follow the risen King of Kings into battle!

He has equipped us with all that we need to win, and He is always at hand to rescue us! Let's be encouraged to keep asking, keep trusting, and keep believing that God will help us in times of trouble through supernatural ways we cannot even begin to imagine.

God Is My Helper in Everything!

There are so many ways that we need God's help: from the small details in our everyday lives, to the huge and traumatic tragedies that can occur without warning. This is where the Holy Spirit comes in to help us! Throughout the Bible it is clear that God is able and willing to help us. Isaiah 41:10 says, "So do not fear, for I am with you; do not be dismayed, for I am your God. I will strengthen you and help you; I will uphold you with my righteous right hand," and verse 13 gets even more personal: "For I am the

LORD, your God, who takes hold of your right hand and says to you, Do not fear; I will help you."

What a beautiful picture of the Lord, your God, *holding your hand* and *helping you*. God comes down to your level—to where you stumble, fall, or feel afraid—holds your hand, and helps you up. This picture brings to mind a father helping his toddler walk, picking her up when she stumbles, and going along with her when she wants to explore. If you observe a toddler you will see how much security holding a parent's hand can bring. In the same way, God in heaven understands that we can be afraid of falling or of that which is still too tricky or difficult for us to do on our own, and He takes hold of our hand, picks us up, and helps us. God longs for us to ask for His help and to call on Him, and He will delight in answering and helping His children.

In 2 Corinthians 6:2 Paul says, "For he says, 'In the time of my favor I heard you, and in the day of salvation I helped you.' I tell you, now is the time of God's favor, now is the day of salvation."

We are able to call on God for help whatever the problem, whether it's not being able to get out of bed in the morning, struggling with paying the mortgage, or being out of relationship with someone dear. There is nothing that God in His mercy cannot help you with.

Control Freak!

But God chose the foolish things of the world to shame the wise; God chose the weak things of the world to shame the strong. (1 Cor. 1:27)

On a program I recently watched, a woman was accused of being a "control freak." Her husband valiantly defended her and explained that as a child she had no safe place, and so the only way she felt safe as an adult was to control everyone and everything—*even him.*

This is true for many women today. For whatever reason, they like—even need—to be in firm control over their lives. Independence is healthy, but using our energy and strength to control situations without God is not. Our own strength is simply not good enough. In the areas that we have no control, it can actually be easier to say, "Lord, I trust You," because there is nothing else to do! How wonderful to know that He is ready to step in and lead us away from trying to do everything with our own effort. Even in the small details of our lives, we need to recognize Jesus as Lord, which means He is the boss. You may not want a boss—and if that's the case, your pride could cause a fall. But God wants us to realize sooner rather than later that we cannot (and weren't designed to) go through life on our own.

We cannot develop a godly character on our own, *without the Holy Spirit.* In John 15:5 Jesus says, "I am the vine; you are the branches. If a man remains in me and I in him, he will bear much fruit; apart from me you can do nothing."

We cannot develop a godly character on our own, without the Holy Spirit. Gentleness and humility help you let go of the need to control. Peace supersedes the need for knowing where you are going at all times. And if you become tempted to pick up the reins, then find a quiet spot and submit yourself to God. Throughout the day continually call on Him to be your helper and boss, and praise Him for being such an amazing Father who leads us gently.

The Holy Spirit Is on Our Side!

In John chapter 16, Jesus speaks about how He must return to the Father so that He can send us the Holy Spirit:

> *However, I am telling you nothing but the truth*
> *when I say it is profitable (good, expedient,*
> *advantageous) for you that I go away. Because*
> *if I do not go away, the Comforter (Counselor,*
> *Helper, Advocate, Intercessor, Strengthener,*
> *Standby) will not come to you [into close*
> *fellowship with you]; but if I go away, I will send*
> *Him to you [to be in close fellowship with you].*
> *(John 16:7 AB)*

Later, after His death and resurrection, Jesus gives the disciples this command: "Do not leave Jerusalem, but wait for the gift my Father promised, which you have heard me speak about. For John baptized with water, but in a few days you will be baptized with the Holy Spirit" (Acts 1:4–5). The disciples are curious about the Holy Spirit—they have only known Jesus so far and find the concept puzzling. Jesus prepares them for all that the Holy Spirit will do, describing Him as an *advocate* three times. *Easton's Bible Dictionary* describes an advocate as "one who pleads another's cause and who helps another by defending or comforting him."[1] How remarkable that Jesus left us the Holy Spirit, who helps, counsels, and comforts us! As our advocate, the Holy Spirit is *on our side*, rooting for us, defending us, helping us, and going ahead of us.

Then Jesus tells us that the Holy Spirit is also *powerful*—"But you will receive power when the Holy Spirit comes on you, and you will be my witnesses in Jerusalem, and in all Judea and Samaria, and to the ends of the earth" (Acts 1:8). So not only is the Holy Spirit kind, good, and gentle, He gives power. Then the God who commissions also enables. Interestingly, in verse 8, Jesus says that when we receive this Holy Spirit we will *be* His witnesses ... not go and *do* some witnessing. As you receive the Holy Spirit's power, God is able to be all that we are not.

At the age of eighteen I was privileged to join a youth program that went into the schools in the UK and Europe to preach the gospel. God opened the doors for me to work with a fantastic team, and I was incredibly eager to go and tell people about His amazing love through the power of the cross!

There was a tiny problem: I was terrified of public speaking. I stuttered and had absolutely no charisma, nor the ability to express myself in an articulate way. I sounded like I was scared of Jesus, not passionate about the way He had changed my life! This continued to be a problem as I regularly went into classrooms with a bright red face and struggled to put a sentence together.

Then one day during a team day at a church in London called Holy Trinity Brompton, the team prayed for me, and some remarkable things started to happen. Physically, I felt incredible power, and afterward I noticed that whenever I needed to speak the timidity had gone! God came in power so that I could *be* His witness. God took the weakness of my natural shyness and gave me His strength to do what I could not do on my own. Being prayed for that day was a powerful, life-altering moment!

I liken it to the time Matt gave me a terrible electric shock. I was actually in labor and in need of some pain relief. He came over to switch on my TENS machine (a device used in labor, which is designed to send electric currents to relieve the pain of contractions), but he had been washing his hands at the sink and forgot to dry them! When he came to help me, I shot off the sofa and right across the room in total agony instead. The shock was powerful but not in a constructive or helpful way! However, the Holy Spirit's power changes you and allows you to go and be what you could not be before: a *witness*.

We are in a supernatural battle fought out on the field of our lives. Sometimes it can feel overwhelming, but we must remember that God is our Helper in every way. His Word and His armor enable us to fight against our negative thoughts, emotions, and doubts. Finally, His Holy Spirit fills, enables, empowers, equips, and commissions us to speak for Him. He calls us to go boldly into the world and into the battle, to proclaim His name and advance His kingdom, for the sake of His glory and the salvation of many souls. *And He doesn't ask us to go alone.*

Whatever troubles you may face—physical, emotional, or spiritual, God is there to help you, with His Spirit, His angels, His power, and His Word.

"There is no one like the God of Jeshurun, who
rides on the heavens to help you and on the

clouds in his majesty. The eternal God is your refuge, and underneath are the everlasting arms."
(Deut. 33:26–27)

Chapter Seven

God Is My Defender

God Defends Me

Defend my cause and redeem me; preserve my life according to your promise. (Ps. 119:154)

We are in a battle, and we have an Enemy. We live in a broken world among broken people, and relationships can cause us much pain and anguish. Yet how precious is it that in the midst of life, we have a God who is our Defender?

God promises us that He will defend us against *accusations*. False accusations always originate from the Enemy and *never* from God. The Devil is known as the "accuser" in Job 2:1 (AB), and in Revelation 12:10 we see how he will be dealt with: "the accuser of our brothers, who accuses them before our God day and night, has been hurled down."

Jesus Himself has been accused by our great Enemy and showed us how to respond. He suffered unjustly and demonstrated how we must hold on to the God who defends, redeems, and judges justly.

Identifying and Responding to Rivals

When the former Spice Girl Posh Spice was introduced to Naomi Campbell, the supermodel reportedly asked her, "Why do they call you Posh?" To which Posh Spice replied, "Why do they call you beautiful?"[1]

Rivalries have always existed between women. We know that they are still alive and well today as the celebrity magazine market thrives on the gossip that the rivalries create, stoking the fire and adding to the problem. Maybe someone tormented you in school, and later you saw that nastiness transferred into the workplace. You may not get along with a member of your family, so much so that you just cannot bear to be near her because she seems so nasty! The thing that we least expect, however, is to find our rival in the church.

In 1 Samuel 1 we meet Hannah, the wife of Elkanah. In verses 5 and 6 we read that the Lord closed Hannah's womb, but Peninnah, Elkanah's second wife, could have children. Every year they all went to the temple to celebrate the Feast of Tabernacles. This festival celebrated God's blessing on the year's crops. So at this time of year Hannah's deep sorrow was all the more profound as the joy, festivity, and feasting to celebrate the year's fruitfulness reminded her of her own barrenness. However, remarkably, Hannah went to the temple year after year. Even in suffering as her prayers seemed unheard, she chose to go to the house of God to cry and plead for a miracle. Yet right in that moment of her greatest vulnerability, her rival came along to increase her grief: "And because the LORD had closed her womb, her rival kept provoking her *in order to irritate her.* This went on year after year. Whenever Hannah went up to the house of the LORD, her rival provoked her till she wept and would not eat" (1 Sam. 1:6–7).

Over a long period of time, Peninnah *deliberately* and *continually* provoked Hannah to tears with her tormenting. As if it wasn't enough that Hannah had to endure years of barrenness; as if it wasn't difficult enough to celebrate when she felt like falling apart; as if it wasn't hard enough to choose to go to the house of the Lord and beg God for a miracle; as if it wasn't tough enough to keep a good attitude—at the moment of her greatest vulnerability, her rival came along to provoke her.

The story of Hannah demonstrates that when you go to pray to God, to consecrate yourself, and commit yourself to Him, your rival is likely to appear. Hannah's rival increased her suffering, "tormented her," and actually taunted her. *What terrible words.* Did she parade her baby past Hannah in the temple? Did she jeer at Hannah's faith in God and her unanswered prayers?

It causes me incredible sadness when I see women hurting one another in the church. Just as one woman tries to become a godly woman of noble character, bringing her pain or worries before the Lord, a rival in her midst can hurt with her words and actions. The Enemy always looks for a quick and immediate way to steal away the word God gave you, or the work He did in your life. Very often the first tool that comes to hand is to bring dissension *in the church*.

Now this is something we don't talk about very often, as it can be difficult to share about our experiences with rivals because they are often very close to us, consider themselves friends, and may even be Christians. However, I am very grateful to Joyce Meyer for sharing the following story, which helped me in my feelings toward my own "rival," and challenged my response.

Joyce spoke about a woman in her church who would regularly come up to her after she had spoken at a meeting and do everything she could to discourage her and make her feel bad. Joyce tried to put up with this for a while, until she decided to bring it to the Lord in prayer: "Lord, what am I going to do about this woman?" As she offered this cry of anger and despair to God she felt Him answer very clearly: "Go and get the nicest thing in your wardrobe, the thing you love the most, and sow it into her life."

Of course, Joyce was horrified!

Why would she do this for a woman who was deliberately discouraging and provoking her? But God used this woman to sharpen Joyce and strengthen her character. Of course, that was not this woman's motivation; she didn't want to make Joyce a better person—rather this woman wanted to hurt her. She delighted in knocking Joyce down. Joyce felt confused but obediently gave away the most precious item from her closet, a fur coat. As she sowed this extravagant gift into this difficult relationship, not only did God bless her obedience, but her act of kindness silenced her tormentor completely.

Our response to unfair treatment and false accusations can deeply impact our character development and change us for good. At times of outrageous treatment at the hands of those who call themselves Christians, or those who call themselves our friends, we need to exercise the commands of Scripture in our lives. We need to ask God what we can sow into the lives of our rivals today—though it may be just a prayer of blessing, it may also be a fur coat!

These acts are not only amazing ways to sow peace but also a powerful method of living in the opposite spirit and ultimately defeating the Enemy's dream of retaliation and dissension in the house of God. God loves it when we persevere through adversity and, in humility, honor Him when we are hurting. He loves it when against all odds we put on love and prefer peace and kind speech.

The first person the Devil spoke to was a woman. He manipulated her to speak his lies to a man. Jesus reversed this curse by constantly speaking *revelation* to women. Jesus told the woman at the well that He was the water of life; He told Martha at the raising of Lazarus that He was the resurrection and the life; and the risen Christ appeared to three women on Easter Sunday and instructed them to tell the disciples the good news.

We still have the same choices today—to listen to and speak the lies of the Enemy, who comes to kill, steal, and destroy; or to listen to and speak the revelation and the truth of God. The Devil was present in the garden of Eden, and we are told he accuses us before the throne of God—but he doesn't always appear as an obvious threat. Therefore, we must constantly guard whom we listen to and what we say. Guard your heart when you go to the temple, and be discerning listeners and speakers of truth and life.

A Gossip Separates Close Friends

A gossip: "A person who habitually spreads intimate or private rumors or facts."[2]

When we feel hurt it is very easy for our mouths to start a fire. The Bible warns of the grave dangers that gossip can cause: "The tongue is a small part of the body, but it makes great boasts. Consider what a great forest is set on fire by a small spark. The tongue also is a fire, a world of evil among the parts of the body. It corrupts the whole person, sets the whole course of his life on fire, and is itself set on fire by hell" (James 3:5–6). Verses 9–11 go on: "With the tongue we praise our Lord and Father, and with it we curse men, who have been made in God's likeness. Out of the same mouth come praise and cursing. My brothers, this should not be. Can both fresh water and salt water flow from the same spring?"

We often talk because we look for sympathy and justice from others. However, this rarely helps. A friend or leader can give you a measure of sympathy, but it is never enough. I know I have nearly driven Matt crazy, trying over and over again to get him to validate my cause or rise up in my defense! Though talking to him may not seem like gossip, if it stirs up the trouble in my heart, then my words and my struggle are better laid down at the feet of my gracious Defender rather than my amazing husband.

So does this mean we can't say anything to anyone? Of course, I would never hide anything in my marriage, but the problem is that talking is unlikely to win you real justice. A better option would be to say, "Can we pray?" When we simply talk, it can fuel anger and hurt as you go over the outrageous thing that person said or did to you again and again.

As you tell other people what happened to you, their angered response brings it all back, or their lack of validation may cause you to seek out yet another ear. It's like reheating a meal. Talking turns the heat back up, and before you know it, the dish is boiling over again. Repeating to others therefore becomes an unhealthy way to spend our time, as it simply stirs us up and causes inner turmoil. Festering on wrong words won't make them right and will not bring us peace. Proverbs has a lot to say on the subject of gossip. Proverbs 18:8 says, "The words of a gossip are like choice morsels; they go down to a man's inmost parts," and Proverbs 26:20 goes on: "Without wood a fire goes out; without gossip a quarrel dies down." Gossip is rather like a double-edged sword—spreading it is dangerous, but so is hearing it. Participating either way is corrupting to our heart and soul. Jesus says in Mark 4:24, "Consider carefully what you hear," because who and what we listen to affects our hearts. So be wise with what you say, but also be wise in what you allow yourself to hear.

Personally, God has been challenging me to not simmer or boil over but to turn the heat down and trust in Him. I have found that by not speaking about something, not allowing my mind to wander, and ultimately, not sinning in the heat of my anger, many, *many* situations have cooled all by themselves. Of course, I'm not talking about repressing things ... that is *not* healthy. But what I am saying is this: What your flesh demands and what the Enemy longs for are not what God requires.

Rather than bring our troubles and problems to other people, we need to bring our petitions to the Lord—the only One who can deal with us in righteousness and justice. Then, as He leads, we can go to the person in grace and seek resolution and peace.

Resolution takes two humble hearts. When the Bible tells us to "put on love," it must be said that we cannot put love on top of negative feelings and unforgiven sin. We need to take that brokenness to

God first, be humble about what we can learn, and then with a freed heart and walking in forgiveness, go to the person.

I am so honored to have a Father that I can go to with everything. All the mess and turmoil can be taken to Him and laid down. He is available *always*. This way, instead of battling a person ourselves, head-to-head, we can shut off the heat and release our frustration to the God who can justify and defend us. He is a safe place for us. He rules and judges fairly, and trusting and obeying Him will bless your relationships more than you could ever imagine.

Facing Unjust Suffering

It is commendable if a man bears up under the pain of unjust suffering because he is conscious of God. (1 Peter 2:19)

When we follow Christ, we will always find a measure of unjust suffering and false accusations in our lives. Peter says in 1 Peter 2:20–21, "If you suffer for doing good and you endure it, this is commendable before God. To this you were called, because Christ suffered for you, leaving you an example, that you should follow in his steps."

If people think wrongly of you because of your accusers, and if you do well before the Lord by refusing to counter their accusations, then this is commendable *before God!* Peter describes Christ's example in verse 23: "When they hurled their insults at him, he did not retaliate; when he suffered, he made no threats." Jesus did not get into a yelling match of accusation and counteraccusation. Rather, He remained silent because "he entrusted himself to him who judges justly" (v. 23).

When we face unjust suffering, or when a person falsely accuses us and we don't know where to turn, we can follow Christ's example and trust in Him who judges justly. We don't have to fight for ourselves, speak for ourselves, or try to obtain justice for ourselves, because the just Judge sees us and will defend us. We only need believe and trust in the promises throughout Scripture that God is willing, able, and in fact, longing to rescue us and defend us.

As we read in Isaiah 30:18 (AB):

> *The Lord [earnestly] waits [expecting, looking,*
> *and longing] to be gracious to you; and therefore*
> *He lifts Himself up, that He may have mercy*
> *on you and show loving-kindness to you. For*
> *the Lord is a God of justice. Blessed (happy,*
> *fortunate, to be envied) are all those who*
> *[earnestly] wait for Him, who expect and look*
> *and long for Him [for his victory, His favor,*
> *His love, His peace, His joy, and His matchless,*
> *unbroken companionship]!*

Receive God's Pity

He will take pity on the weak and needy. (Ps. 72:13)

God interacts with us in love, mercy, and compassion, not in anger or wrath. Psalm 103 says, "As a father pities his children, so the LORD pities those who fear Him" (v. 13 NKJV). When I read this, I feel overwhelmed with comfort. I suddenly realize that God actually pities us! I'd only ever seen pity as a bad thing, something to reject from others, and almost a kind of weakness. Actually, it's *self*-pity that is the negative thing.

If we don't adequately receive God's pity and care for us, then self-pity rises up and consumes us as we're tormented by the wrong done to us. Self-pity wrongly causes us to withdraw into ourselves and wallow in our own troubles.

On the other hand, God's compassion frees us! When we realize that His pity is enough, we don't need to seek sympathy from others because in its place we have something much more powerful and comforting. The definition of *pity* is "sympathetic or kindly sorrow evoked by the suffering, distress, or misfortune of another, often leading one to give relief or aid or to show mercy."[3] Pity is having compassion beyond just saying, "Oh well, sorry about that." Pity understands, listens, and weeps with the suffering of another—and seeks to relieve it. It is sorrow with love, compassion with a tear.

As we noted earlier, when we look for empathy in the wrong place we can gossip, embellish, or stretch the facts because we are looking for someone to rescue, defend, or sympathize with us. God sees every single detail concerning your situation, and where you have been genuinely wronged, misunderstood, or mistreated. He pities you; His heart tears, and He is moved to act. He has compassion for those who fear Him when they suffer unjustly. I love the fact that Scripture says God is like a Father to His children. In the same way that parents don't love one child any more or less than another yet still empathize with each child's point of view, so God sees each of our circumstances.

Vengeance Is Mine: God Is the Just Judge

He will judge your people in righteousness, your afflicted ones with justice. (Ps. 72:2)

Knowing that God cares for us in this way is such a relief. It's a gift! I feel free not having to fight my case or defend my cause. If we put as much effort into pursuing peace as we do in trying to defend ourselves, the world would be an incredibly harmonious place. You see, God examines what is going on, and with a full understanding, He works on our behalf. He sees the truth in all its complexity. Sometimes our perception of someone or an account of a story can be a warped version of the truth. God sees both sides. Someone once told me that in every disagreement there is your story, their story, and the truth! God will work out His perfect justice in each circumstance according to the truth and according to our attitude.

God is very clear about one thing: *He is the only just judge.* Romans 12:19 says, "Do not take revenge, my friends, but leave room for God's wrath, for it is written, 'It is mine to avenge, I will repay,' says the Lord." In Hebrews 10:30 the Amplified Bible says, "For we know Him Who said, Vengeance is Mine [retribution and the meting out of full justice rest with Me]; I will repay [I will exact the compensation], says the Lord. And again, the Lord will judge and determine and solve and settle the cause and the cases of His people."

The phrase "I will exact the compensation" meticulously describes how fair God is. God deals with people in His infinite mercy and grace, and in so doing He will find the perfect way to judge us and bring us to repentance for the sin committed. Psalm 119:7 says, "I will praise and give thanks to You with uprightness of heart when I learn [by sanctified experiences] Your righteous judgment [Your decisions against and punishments for particular lines of thought and conduct]" (AB). Verses 9 and 10 go on: "How shall a young man cleanse his way? By taking heed and keeping watch [on himself] according to Your word [conforming his life to it]. With my whole heart have I sought You, inquiring for and of You and yearning for You; Oh, let me not wander or step aside [either in ignorance or willfully] from Your commandments" (AB).

I think this verse is stunning. It reminds us that to take revenge would be to stray from God's commands. In seeking justice for ourselves we can wander from trust and try to become self sufficient, believing we have to prove our own innocence or plead our own cause. The psalmist remembers that he can depend on God's righteous judgment always. It is also a continual reminder to me to seek God so that I do not wander into ignorance or sin but stay faithful to His commands for dealing with unjust suffering.

This is often easier said than done!

First of all, let humility truly be tested in you. Repent of any pride, gossip, or self-righteousness, and any possible part that you may have played. Psalm 139:23–24 is useful in leading us into true self-examination and confession: "Search me, O God, and know my heart; test me and know my anxious thoughts. See if there is any offensive way in me, and lead me in the way everlasting."

So God sees us, pities us, and can powerfully use our difficult circumstances to purify our hearts and refine our character. This is *so* not pleasant at the time, but as we trust God, the true and only just

Judge of men, we can hold on to His promise that He will lift us up and work for good in our lives.

Forgive as God Forgave You

He will make your righteousness shine like the dawn, the justice of your cause like the noonday sun. (Ps. 37:6)

When Jesus teaches us how to pray, He focuses particularly on forgiving others:

> *"If you forgive people their trespasses [their reckless and willful sins, leaving them, letting them go, and giving up resentment], your heavenly Father will also forgive you. But if you do not forgive others their trespasses [their reckless and willful sins, leaving them, letting them go, and giving up resentment], neither will your Father forgive you your trespasses." (Matt. 6:14-15 AB)*

If you do not forgive a wrong done to you, it can be very much like torture of the heart. In this situation we can hold on to resentment, to the wrongs done to us, and to the words spoken over us. Withholding forgiveness from others means God's forgiveness cannot reach us either—and so a barrier is built up between our Creator and us. This barrier is entirely of our own making and can affect the way God hears our prayers and affects our future.

Forgiving someone releases you from the memory of whatever was done or said. It does not mean that what that person did was okay. Look at how the disciples dealt with the fallout from the betrayal of Judas. Peter stood up and addressed the remaining disciples. He acknowledged what had happened—the wickedness of Judas' betrayal and horrific end—but drew a line under it and reappointed a twelfth apostle.

Acknowledge the wrong done to you, and then let it go—move on and forgive as you were forgiven.

Not forgiving leads to crippling bitterness. The story of Cain and Abel shows us the devastation that bitterness toward God can cause. Cain's offering was not pleasing to God, and his heart became bitter. What's interesting about this story is that right before this, God spoke to Cain in pity and love. He asks Cain in Genesis 4:6–7, "Why are you angry, and why has your face fallen? If you do well, will you not be accepted? And if you do not do well, sin is crouching at the door. Its desire is for you, but you must rule over it" (ESV).

Like the example of Cain, there seems to be a connection between our response—or reaction—to God, and our falling into sin. We see that God is Cain's greatest cheerleader.

"Don't do it!" God says. "There's still a way out. You can still change your heart and do well." God is not against Cain. *He is for him!* God knows that the condition of Cain's heart is the most crucial thing and so He challenges Cain to do the right thing. There was still time. He didn't have to fall into sin. He didn't have to lose relationship with God, who was fighting for him, fighting to break through his unforgiving heart. Cain didn't have to live out a life suffering the consequences of his poor choices. But he did. And sin was right there waiting for him, feeding him, and luring him into defeat. His anger turned to bitterness, which consumed him when he killed his brother Abel.

Unresolved anger against another human being—and, even more so, against God—has the potential to devastate the course of your entire life. Just look at Cain! He spent the rest of his days wandering in the wilderness.

Look to God, who cheers you on and calls you away from sin and into love. Trust Him and begin relationship with Him again. *Be determined.* Extinguish any anger over sins you haven't forgiven (by forgiving), and rectify any barrier in your life through Jesus.

Blessing Your Enemies

I tell you: Love your enemies and pray for those who persecute you. (Matt. 5:44)

Once we confess our sins, put our trust in God, and forgive our enemies, it is time to bless them! As we saw in Joyce Meyer's fur coat story, blessing those who curse us can have a profound impact both on us and on the person we seek to bless.

I have a friend in London whose aggressive neighbor verbally abused her out in the street one day. Her neighbor was a large, angry drug addict, and, of course, he knew where she lived. You did not want to get on the wrong side of this man! As he screamed and swore at her in the street, he finished his tirade by telling her that on top of all the problems he had with her, his sister had died that week.

My friend was deeply shaken, but she decided to pray about her response. *Go and buy him a plant*, she felt the Lord tell her. Obediently, she went to a little florist shop, and with the help of her little boy, who had witnessed the tirade, she chose a potted plant for her neighbor, wrapped it up, and wrote him a card. Nervously, she walked down the road and found him outside the house. She didn't have to say a word as the simple blessing of a potted plant melted the heart of this great big aggressive man and almost reduced him to tears.

People in pain often inflict pain on others, either knowingly or unknowingly. We must learn how to identify the people in our lives who behave as if they are our enemies, or those to whom we react in a negative way, and ask the Lord to bless them. As we do, the Lord will work in our characters in a refining way, shaving down our pride and uprooting the sin buried deep within our hearts, challenging us and enabling us to empathize with and even love those enemies who persecute us. Never let the accuser throw up a barrier between you and God!

"Bless those who persecute you; bless and do not curse," Paul says in Romans 12:14. He goes on:

> *Rejoice with those who rejoice; mourn with those*
> *who mourn. Live in harmony with one another.*
> *Do not be proud, but be willing to associate*
> *with people of low position. Do not be conceited.*
> *Do not repay anyone evil for evil. Be careful to*
> *do what is right in the eyes of everybody. If it is*
> *possible, as far as it depends on you, live at peace*

with everyone. Do not take revenge, my friends,
but leave room for God's wrath, for it is written,
"It is mine to avenge; I will repay," says the Lord.
(vv. 15–19)

So when we've been hurt, let's quickly come to God and receive His amazing, freeing pity—and let the blessing of our enemies and our rivals begin!

Chapter Eight

GOD IS MY RESTORER

A Time of Devastation

To you, O LORD, I call, for fire has devoured the open pastures and flames have burned up all the trees of the field. (Joel 1:19)

Have you ever read the book of Joel? Initially it's seriously scary stuff. The people of Judah had fallen far from God and lived in continual sin with a gross lack of repentance. The prophet Joel had to bring what was initially a strong prophetic word of judgment from God to the people of Judah, and the first chapter contains a damning indictment to God's people.

As a result of their sin and rebellion, God sent a time of suffering to the land of Judah. The people suffered *four* different plagues of locusts, and as a result, crops, livestock, and people perished. During this time there was nothing to eat, neither crops from the field nor from the tree, and there was nothing to drink, much to the distress of the drunkards of the time!

The best way for us to understand exactly what this would

mean for us is to think of every single supermarket shelf in our city completely empty. There would be no way for us to buy or obtain food. We would all be very hungry and desperate. Right now in East Africa, 23 million people face severe hunger and destitution as a result of drought over the past five years. The situation is made even worse by high food prices and conflict. Similarly, in Zimbabwe the supermarkets are empty due to massive economic problems. There is no choice but to try to grow your own food.

As the people of Judah experience this dramatic shortage of food, Joel interprets this destruction as divine judgment and urges the people of Judah to repent (confess their sin and say sorry to God), telling them that God wants to bring immense restoration to their extreme devastation.

For me, that time of devastation and disaster was my childhood. For years the Devil used my circumstances to make me believe I was vile and worthless.

My dad was broken, and as a result of his own pain, he physically abused our family. For years we lived in fear, under an atmosphere of control. In my childhood home many doors had fist holes punched through them, and several of the walls bore impressions of our heads. For a season we went through telephones the way most people go through bread and milk. When it got bad my mum or I would get smacked with the telephone as we tried to call for help.

On top of this, kids bullied me at school. Several times kids chased me onto the school bus with eggs and flour, and then I found find myself bullied on my way home on the bus by the children from my council estate. It was lonely and harsh. I am so thankful we were brought up going to church, because it was eventually the church that would come to my rescue.

After seventeen years of physical violence I became so resilient that after coming home one day to find my mum sobbing from an altercation with my father, I called the church. My dad was forced to leave, and my mum finally had the support to move on. We packed up his things, and he began a new life without us.

A few days after she made that decision, but before we had the sense to change the locks, I was at home by myself when I heard a noise on the landing. My dad had brought a male "friend" around to "discuss" the matter with me. As the man held me up against the wall by the scruff of my neck and shook me and blamed me, my dad looked on, emotionless.

I don't think I've ever felt so disgraced and rejected all at once. My childhood was like that great army of locusts, destroying my innocence and devastating my future hope.

A Call to Repentance and Prayer

Declare a holy fast; call a sacred assembly. Summon the elders and all who live in the land to the house of the LORD your God, and cry out to the LORD. (Joel 1:14)

Joel calls the whole nation to repentance over the state the country finds itself in. Drunkards, farmers, and priests alike (Joel 1:5, 11, 13) are called to mourn over the devastation of the land. It would appear that the nation of Judah lived in a time of blatant sin and disobedience, but the only *specific* sin mentioned in the book is drunkenness. Drunkenness suggests a self-indulgent lifestyle, pursued by those who value material things over the spiritual. The drunkenness obviously led to laziness, as Joel has to call the drunkards to wake up in verse 5: "Wake up, you drunkards, and weep! Wail, all you drinkers of wine, wail because of the new wine, for it has been snatched from your lips."

In His righteous judgment, God removed the very thing that led to sin and self-indulgence in order to call the sinners to repentance. Becoming drunk is a symptom of other underlying problems and is often a way of denying the truth or blocking out the reality of sin, despair, and hurt in our lives. Yet God says, "Wake up! Come to your senses and look at where your attempts to save yourself have gotten you. Look at it, and wail and weep. Come to Me and ask for forgiveness, and I will have mercy."

Once my dad finally left our lives, it was amazing to be free; however, emotionally I wasn't free at all. The locusts had left, but the destruction they caused was still apparent. I held a deep anger inside my heart and an insane fatherless grief that followed me everywhere. I felt stripped of hope and emotionally crippled. I struggled with my self-image and covered my body in shame by day and escaped and got drunk at night.

As a child it felt like there was no safe place. Yet, upon reflection, God was always, *always* there for me. He provided in my childhood what would be the saving grace in my adult life—Sunday school, youth group, Christian camps, and ultimately a vibrant church to run to when my world came crashing down. When I look back, I see that while I felt helpless and distraught at times, God faithfully provided an outlet for me and built the safety net that would save me. I was able to sing, dance, laugh, learn, enjoy friends, and know God in it all. Even in the darkest times when I would go to church on Sunday smelling of cigarettes and alcohol, feeling disgusted with myself, I was being called by a God who saves!

One of the most amazing things about my church was the prayer ministry after the service. During this prayer time someone would pray for you and try to help you experience the supernatural power of the Holy Spirit. After being prayed for one particular time I felt so much power that I fell down. I've been shocked before, but this was different. It was painless and far more powerful.

As I let go of what felt like thousands of pent-up tears, this amazing promise from Joel began to take shape in my life, and I repented and returned to God. I praised God for the cross, and I fully understood it for the first time in that moment. I repented of my anger, my lack of forgiveness toward others, and my sinful search for acceptance. Instead of grief there was joy, instead of shame there was freedom, and instead of rejection there was peace.

God Saves and Restores You

Rend your heart and not your garments. Return to the LORD your God, for he is gracious and compassionate, slow to anger and abounding in love, and he relents from sending calamity. (*Joel 2:13*)

After calling Judah to return to Him and repent through the prophet Joel, God reminds His people of His loving nature and provides a way out, a sumptuous, undeserved plan of recovery, restoration, and rescue.

In the same way, God wants *your* heart and *your* undivided love, loyalty, and attention. As we come to Him and repent of our sin— our selfishness, our unforgiveness, our bitterness, and our attempts to save our own souls—He not only forgives us, but He heals and restores us.

It felt like I went forward for prayer at every church meeting over the next few years! I prayed with skillful counselors, and during those encounters with the Holy Spirit I received healing and hope. God replaced every poured-out prayer, tear, and memory with good things. He restored my life. Jesus not only called me to repentance and saved me from my own actions and pain, but He healed and restored all that had been lost and stolen from me. I emerged ready to live for His glory!

After the call to repent in chapter 1, Joel gives a threefold call to joy addressed to the land, the wild animals, and the people in chapter 2: "Be glad, O people of Zion, rejoice in the LORD your God, for he has given you the autumn rains in righteousness. He sends you abundant showers, both autumn and spring rains, as before" (Joel 2:23).

From a farming perspective, the autumn rains were intended to replenish the land from a drought-filled summer, and the spring rains were for future growth. To have both at the same time requires God's supernatural intervention into the natural realm.

In the same way, spiritually, we see a supernatural promise from

God not just to revive and quench the thirst of a barren land, but also to cause it to grow and flourish at the same time.

God Restores You

I will repay you for the years the locusts have eaten. (Joel 2:25)

Joel mentions several different types of locust plagues. In chapter 1, verse 4 we see references to the great locusts, young locusts, other locusts, and the locust swarm. Each form of locust causes various degrees of devastation.

The immature or young locusts start by gnawing off whatever they can find. Then the locusts begin to swarm as they mature, causing damage through their vast numbers, eating their own body weight in vegetation in a day. A locust swarm might consist of anywhere from a million to a billion locusts a day, and they can literally block out the light of the sun because of their number. Once the swarm moves on, other types of locusts come through and devour whatever is left. These small creatures show no mercy and leave nothing behind.

So let's apply this passage to our lives spiritually. God says to us, whatever locust has plagued you, whatever has been stolen, damaged, or destroyed by the Enemy, by others, or even by your own hands, *can be restored to you.*

Maybe the great locust stripped away everything precious in your life in the form of a tragedy or great struggle. Perhaps a swarm of locusts ravaged your life in the form of annoying problems or difficulties that came all at once and overwhelmed you simply by their number. Maybe you feel that the locust of depression has depleted your life of joy and hope, causing you to shrink back and give up. Perhaps another locust caused you physical pain in some way.

Whatever happened to you, Jesus is able to restore to you *all* that the locusts have eaten. Everything the Enemy took, all that circumstances have inflicted upon you, the times you have messed up—Jesus can recover everything stolen and lost in your life.

The Lord Renews You

The threshing floors will be filled with grain; the vats will overflow with new wine and oil. (Joel 2:24)

As Joel calls the people to gladness and rejoicing in chapter 2, he describes the amazing changes unfolding as a result of God's blessing. The pastures are turning green, the trees are bearing fruit, and the land is plentiful again. *Yet there is more!* Not only will the people's food and land be restored, but their faith will be restored: "You will have plenty to eat, until you are full, and you will praise the name of the LORD your God, who has worked wonders for you; never again will my people be shamed. Then you will know that I am in Israel, that I am the LORD your God" (Joel 2:26–27).

This is a message of restoration and hope for anyone in any difficult circumstance, great or small, self-inflicted or inflicted by another. God makes worn-out, discouraged, and destroyed things brand-new. In fact His specialties often begin with the prefix *re*, which means "again" or "anew." He *re-news*, He *re-wards*, He *re-deems*, *re-fines*, brings *re-compense, re-surrects, re-stores, re-vives, re-leases,* and of course, He teaches us to *re-pent.*

So, what does this mean for the brokenhearted and desperate?

Restoration Sings!

Everyone who calls on the name of the LORD will be saved. (Joel 2:32)

So—hold on, because the *blessing of restoration* is coming. Hold on in times of discouragement, dryness, and weariness. Hold on when it feels like the Enemy destroyed your hope and took all that is precious to you. Galatians 6:7–9 says,

> *Do not be deceived: God cannot be mocked. A man reaps what he sows. The one who sows to please his sinful nature, from that nature will reap destruction; the one who sows to please the Spirit, from the Spirit will reap eternal life. Let us not become weary in doing good, for at the proper time we will reap a harvest if we do not give up.*

What an encouragement to hold on through times of trial and to persevere for the time and season of reversal!

Joel sums it up in chapter 2, verse 27, by saying, "Then you will know that I am the LORD your God, and that there is no other; never again will my people be shamed."

This is the banner under which we worship. We can praise Him with a confidence that our hope in Him will not be disappointed— "No one whose hope is in you will ever be put to shame" (Ps. 25:3). What that means is that we don't have to bear the shame of disappointed hopes. He is who He says He is. He is faithful and good. We hope. We draw near. We return. We repent. We receive. Restoration sings.

Whatever has been lost, the book of Joel reminds us that God is a God of mercy. Our response to His amazing mercy and grace can only be a sacrifice of praise and worship. Sing of His goodness, sing of His marvelous deeds, and sing of His salvation in your life. Proclaim to your soul, the heavens, your friends, and the world that our God reigns in Zion. He dwells with His people in their hearts, and our hope will *never* be put to shame.

Remembrance

By Matt Maher and Matt Redman

Oh how could it be
That my God would welcome me
Into this mystery
Say, "take this bread, take this wine,"
Now the simple made divine
For any to receive

By Your mercy we come to Your table
By Your grace You are making us faithful

Lord, we remember You
And remembrance leads us to worship
And as we worship You
Our worship leads to communion
We respond to Your invitation
We remember You

See His body, His blood
Know that He has overcome
Every trial we will face
None too lost to be saved
None too broken or ashamed
All are welcome in this place

Dying, You destroyed our death
Rising, You restored our life
Lord Jesus, come in glory
Lord Jesus come in glory[1]

Never Forgotten, Forever Loved

Joel called the people of Judah to repentance, and they turned to the Lord in the midst of a terrible environmental and humanitarian crisis. They lifted their eyes up from the earth and from their surroundings, and they called out to the Lord. In His mercy He heard them from heaven, responded, answered their prayers, and restored them and their land to a place of incredible abundance.

Life will throw us many curveballs. The circumstances may make it appear as though God has forgotten you, but He sees you, hears you, has compassion for you, and always burns with love for you. He is faithful. Trust in Him through whatever life throws at you, honor Him by believing that He is good and He could never forget *you*.

Trust, believe, and know that your God is with you. Your name is engraved on the palm of His hand. You are His. Never forgotten, forever loved. God hears you. God loves you. God knows your name! Always and forever, amen!

> *Praise the LORD, all you nations;*
> *extol him, all you peoples.*

> *For great is his love toward us,*
> *and the faithfulness of the LORD endures*
> *forever. (Ps. 117)*

STUDY GUIDE

Chapter One: God Knows My Name

Reading

Read Isaiah 43:1–4 together.

Questions for Discussion

1. This chapter is concerned with the deeply personal nature of our relationship with God. How do you think you could take steps to deepen and strengthen that relationship and respond to God's call on your life?

Step One:

Step Two:

Step Three:

Step Four:

Step Five:

2. "I know you by name, you are Mine" (Isa. 43:1, author's paraphrase). What implications does this verse have for our understanding of our relationship with God and for our lives?

Impact on what I think about God:

Impact on my relationship with God:

Impact on my life:

3. "Since you are precious and honored in my sight, and because I love you" (Isa. 43:4). How does this definition of you and declaration of love for you from the Lord of heaven and earth change the way you see yourself? How does it change the way you speak and act?

How I used to see myself:

How I see myself now:

This is going to change how I speak in the following ways:

This is going to change how I act in the following ways:

4. When did you last feel heard and understood by God? Remind yourself of how He spoke to you by sharing with the group and making a note of it here:

5. Now ask God to speak to you again. Be specific in your request, share your prayer with the group, and keep a record of it below:

Prayer

Lord Jesus, King of Kings, Lord of Lords, Maker of heaven and earth,

Thank You for calling me by name, for loving me, making me, and treasuring me. Your grace and mercy astound and amaze me. May I live a life of gratitude for all You have done. Take my life and use it for Your glory. May I live as a child of the King, secure in my knowledge of Your love for me. May I bring Your love, mercy, and grace to others and give glory back to You.

In Jesus' holy name I pray,

Amen.

Chapter Two: God Knows My Past

Reading

Read 1 John 1:5 and 1 John 2:11 together.

Questions for Discussion

1. What is your past? What have you been rescued from? In what way is it releasing and comforting to know that God knows your past and still loves you?

2. Is there any part of your past that still holds you back or makes you feel unworthy? Give it to God in repentance and thank Him for forgiving you.

3. It can be easy to slip into the habit of casually judging others on what they say or do, or even on appearances. In what ways do you find yourself judging others?

4. How could you change your attitudes, thoughts, and words to make them more loving? Ask God to help you do this.

Prayer

Please pray the Lord's Prayer from Matthew 6:9–13.

> *Our Father in heaven*
> *hallowed be your name*
> *your kingdom come,*
> *your will be done*
> *on earth as it is in heaven.*
> *give us today our daily bread.*
> *forgive us our debts,*
> *as we also have forgiven our debtors.*
> *and lead us not into temptation,*
> *but deliver us from the evil one,*
> *for yours is the kingdom and the power and the glory*
> *forever. Amen.*

Chapter Three: God Shapes My Character

Reading
Read Matthew 25:14–30 together.

Questions for Discussion

1. What gifts have you been given? Are you using them? If not, what is preventing you from using them to further God's kingdom?

2. Both David and the faithful servants (in Matthew 25:14–30) are rewarded for their diligence and trustworthiness in using what they were given. What aspects of your character require the most work and attention? How do you think you could develop these most effectively?

3. "Blessed is the man who trusts in the LORD, whose confidence is in him" (Jer. 17:7). Are there any parts of your life with which you are still fearful of trusting God? Or have you drifted along and simply forgotten to commit your path to the Lord? Spend some time committing your ways to Him and trusting Him with anything you may be afraid to commit to Him.

4. What are the desires of your heart? Spend some time thinking about this. Often they are buried deep in our subconscious and not verbalized. If you can, verbalize them in prayer to Jesus and give them to Him, asking Him to use them for His kingdom, to lead and direct your paths.

Prayer

Please pray together the benediction from Numbers 6:24–26:

> *The LORD bless you*
> *and keep you;*
> *the LORD make his face shine upon you*
> *and be gracious to you;*
> *the LORD turn his face toward you*
> *and give you peace.*

Amen.

Chapter Four: God Sees My Choices

Reading

Read Joshua 24:14–15 together.

Questions for Discussion

1. If your journey of faith is a race toward Jesus and away from the Enemy, how do you feel you are doing? Take a moment to consider how you are running in your lane. Do you feel enthusiastic or tired, or are you jogging along nicely?

2. What is your specific need at this time in your race? Take a moment to ask God to provide it.

3. What, if anything, is hindering you at the moment? What are the "gods your forefathers worshiped" that you need to throw away? Bring these things to the cross of Jesus and leave them there in prayer.

4. In what ways can you choose to honor God in your life right now?

5. What bold steps of faith could you start to take in your life to serve Christ and His kingdom?

Prayer

Lord Jesus, today I choose to fix my eyes on You, to run toward You and away from all the sin that so easily entangles. Forgive me when I stumble and fall, and give me the grace to get up and keep running toward You. May You grant me all that I need, may Your Word sustain me and Your Spirit empower me.

I choose today to follow You and to honor You with my words, my deeds, my actions, and my choices. I want to step out in faith and honor You in everything I do. Give me the faith to run my race with courage, determination, and boldness.

In Jesus' name,

Amen.

Chapter Five: God Has Not Forgotten Me

Reading
Please read together Isaiah 49:8–16

Questions for Discussion

1. What are you waiting for at this moment in your life?

2. What needs are currently troubling you? What do you need the great I Am to be in your life right now?

3. Are there areas in your life where you doubt God's ability or goodness? Ask the Lord to increase your faith in these areas, and ask Him to provide what you need.

4. This week, practice using Scripture in different situations that you face. Please reference the Scriptures on pages 110–112 to get you going.

Prayer

Please pray this prayer from Psalm 62:5–8.

> *Let all that I am wait quietly before God, for my hope is in him. He alone is my rock and my salvation, my fortress where I will not be shaken. My victory and honor come from God alone. He is my refuge, a rock where no enemy can reach me. O my people, trust in him at all times. Pour out your heart to him, for God is our refuge. (Ps. 62:5–8 NLT)*

Amen.

Chapter Six: God Is My Helper

Reading

Read Psalm 91 together.

Questions for Discussion

1. When have you known God as your Helper in your life?

2. In what ways do you need God to help you now?

3. The relationship between our attitude toward God and His response is remarkable. In what ways can you choose to be more trusting and honoring of God in your life?

4. Are there any areas in your life in which you have gone ahead with a good idea without waiting for the Holy Spirit to enable you?

5. Ask the Holy Spirit to come and fill your life with His power and enabling. Spend some time waiting for Him.

Prayer

Please pray together from Ephesians 3:14–21.

> *For this reason I kneel before the Father, from*
> *whom his whole family in heaven and on earth*
> *derives its name. I pray that out of his glorious*
> *riches he may strengthen you with power through*
> *his Spirit in your inner being, so that Christ may*
> *dwell in your hearts through faith. And I pray*
> *that you, being rooted and established in love,*
> *may have power, together with all the saints, to*
> *grasp how wide and long and high and deep is*
> *the love of Christ, and to know this love that*
> *surpasses knowledge—that you may be filled to*
> *the measure of all the fullness of God. Now to*
> *him who is able to do immeasurably more than*
> *all we ask or imagine, according to his power*
> *that is at work within us, to him be glory in*
> *the church and in Christ Jesus throughout all*
> *generations, for ever and ever! Amen. (Eph.*
> *3:14–21)*

Chapter Seven: God Is My Defender

Reading

Read Isaiah 30:18–21 together.

Questions for Discussion

1. At the end of all things, we will all be judged before the Lord, both those who have caused unjust suffering and those who have suffered from it. Let us put our hearts in order and not judge, lest we be judged ourselves. Ask the Lord to search your heart to see if there are any areas of unconfessed sin or sins against you that you haven't yet forgiven, that you need to repent of.

2. How do you need the Lord to defend you in your life at the moment?

3. "Forgive us our sins as we forgive those who sin against us" (Luke 11:4 NLT). Is there anyone that you have not forgiven in your life? Spend a few moments asking the Holy Spirit to search your heart and shine a light on any sins that you haven't forgiven. Forgiveness is an act of will. Thank God that He has forgiven you your sins,

accept His forgiveness of you, and release forgiveness to those who have hurt you or wronged you. Then bless them!

4. Do you have a rival, or can you think of a person who brings out the worst in you? Pray for and bless that person now.

5. Facing unjust suffering and being obedient to God requires us to trust God to defend us and wait for His righteous judgment. This can be fairly difficult to do! What practical steps can you take in your thought life and prayer life that ensure you leave vengeance to God?

Prayer

Thank You, Lord, that You are a God of justice who longs to show mercy and grace to us. Thank You that You are our great Defender against the Enemy, other people, and unjust suffering. Thank You that You see all we are going through and that You have compassion and pity on us. Help us to have compassion and pity on others who are likewise going through a time of trial or suffering. We ask that You would help us to bless our enemies and that You would use times of frustration, suffering, and trials to make us more like Jesus. Forgive us when we hurt others, and forgive us when we fall into gossip or self-pity. Give us the strength and grace to trust in You, lean on You, and depend on You at all times and in all things for Your perfect judgment and grace.

In Jesus' name,

Amen.

Chapter Eight: God Is My Restorer

Reading

Read Joel 2:23–27 together.

Questions for Discussion

1. In the light of the fact that, as John 10:10 tells us, the Enemy "comes ... to steal and kill and destroy," what do you feel has been stolen from you in your life? Did the circumstances cause you to wonder whether God had forgotten you?

2. In Joel 2:25 God says, "I will repay you for the years the locusts have eaten." What does that verse mean in your life today?

3. God promises not just to repay you, but also to restore and renew you. What would that look like in your life, spiritually, today?

4. Worship is a helpful and appropriate response to times of trial and suffering as well as a natural response to what Jesus achieved for us on the cross and the restoration and revival of our lives that He

brings about. It is both a discipline and a delight. Talk about how worshipping through suffering is helpful to your faith, and how it is beneficial in the good times.

Prayer

Father God, there are times when we have felt that things have been taken away and stolen from us by the Enemy. Thank You that You sent Your Son Jesus to redeem our lives, to restore us, revive us, and renew us. Thank You for never forgetting us, no matter what our circumstances may tell us. Thank You for always loving us. We praise You for who You are, for all You have done and all You will do in our lives.

In Jesus' name,

Amen.

NOTES

Chapter One

1. George Maslin, "Shaftsbury Christian Centre, 1844 to 2007," *Records from the Deptford Ragged School,* Princess Louise Institute. Used with permission.

2. *NIV Study Bible* (London: Hodder & Stoughton, 1998), 915 (study notes).

3. Tom Marshall, *Right Relationships* (Chichester, UK: Sovereign World, 2000), 55.

Chapter Three

1. Frank Sinatra, "My Way," © 1969 Reprise Records.

Chapter Four

1. David Wright, Sinclair Ferguson, J. I. Packer, eds., *The New Dictionary of Theology* (Westmont, IL: InterVarsity Press, 1988), 246.

Chapter Six

1. *Easton's Bible Dictionary,* s.v., "Advocate."

Chapter Seven

1. *The Sunday Times,* August 23, 2009.
2. *The American Heritage Dictionary of the English Language*, 4th ed., s.v., "Gossip."
3. Ibid., s.v., "Pity."

Chapter Eight

1. Matt Maher and Matt Redman, "Remembrance," © 2009 Thank you Music / Sixsteps Records (lyrics taken from the English translation of the Memorial Acclamation for the Roman Missal © 1973). Used with permission.

To download Beth Redman's song
"GOD KNOWS MY NAME,"
written exclusively for this book, visit:
www.davidccook.com/redman24661

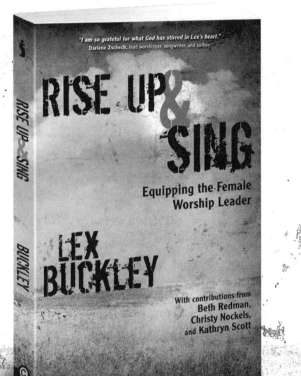